Performance Research Associates'

Delivering Knock Your Socks Off Service

Third Edition Revisions by Ron Zemke

AMACOM
American Management Association

New York • Atlanta • Brussels • Buenos Aires • Chicago • London • Mexico City
San Francisco • Shanghai • Tokyo • Toronto • Washington, D. C.

Special discounts on bulk quantities of AMACOM
books are available to corporations, professional
associations, and other organizations. For details,
contact Special Sales Department, AMACOM,
a division of American Management Association,
1601 Broadway, New York, NY 10019.
Tel.: 212-903-8316. Fax: 212-903-8083.
Web site: www. amacombooks.org

This publication is designed to provide accurate and
authoritative information in regard to the subject matter
covered. It is sold with the understanding that the publisher is
not engaged in rendering legal, accounting, or other
professional service. If legal advice or other expert assistance
is required, the services of a competent professional person
should be sought.

Library of Congress Cataloging-in-Publication Data
Zemke, Ron.
Delivering knock your socks off service / by Ron Zemke.—3rd ed.
        p. cm.
        Rev. ed. of: Delivering knock your socks off service / Kristin
Anderson,
        Ron Zemke. 1998.
        Includes index.
    ISBN 0-8144-0765-X
        1. Customer services. I. Anderson, Kristin. 1962- Delivering knock
your socks off service. II. Title.
HF5415.5 .Z4593 2002
658.8′ 12—dc21   2002011115

DELIVERING KNOCK YOUR SOCKS OFF SERVICE® AND CUSTOMER FROM HELL®
are registered trademarks of Performance Research Associates, Inc.

Artwork © 2003 John Bush

Printing number

10 9 8 7 6 5 4 3

Contents

Preface

What You Do Is Critically Important

It's not enough to merely satisfy the customer; customers must be "delighted"—- surprised by having their needs not just met, but exceeded.
—A. Blanton Godfrey

Serving customers. The two words cover so much. Answering questions. Solving problems. Untangling corporate logjams. Fixing what's broken and finding what's lost. Soothing the irate and reassuring the timid. And time after time, performing the business equivalent of pulling a rabbit out of a hat: Matching people who do business with you with just the right products, services, and solutions.

Not too long ago, working in customer service was just about as thankless a job as a person could find. Sales? That was a job with a future. Marketing? Now there was a title with some prestige. Advertising? What mystique! The Internet—really cool! But customer service? Backwater. A burden. A career path to nowhere. Fellow employees looked down their noses at "those people who deal with whining customers." And customers—well, they mostly seemed to see customer service representative as a title for not very bright people who woke up most mornings, looked in the mirror, grinned wide, and said to their reflections, "This is going to be a fun day. I'm going to go down there and annoy the first 217 people I talk to." And then did just that. Not exactly positive images.

In the late 1990s, about the time of the dot-com debacle, professional business watchers began to relearn something important. They discovered that organizations that had dedicated themselves to working hard at giving their customers superior service were producing better financial results. These organizations grew faster and were more profitable than the organizations that were still working as hard as they could to give their customers as little as possible, whether online, over the phone, or face to face. In short, companies that emphasized total customer service were starting to make more money and keep customers longer than companies that didn't.

Researchers also started to notice that highly successful service organizations had lower marketing costs, fewer upset and complaining customers, and more repeat business—customers were "voting with their feet" and beating a path back to the doors of the companies that served them well. What's more, good service had internal rewards: Employee turnover and absenteeism were lower and morale and job satisfaction higher in these same organizations. Companies that asked employees to make customers happy had happier employees.

Organizations that focused on superior customer service turned out to be all-around better, more successful companies than those that treated customers like the enemy and customer service as either a grudging afterthought or a necessary evil.

Almost overnight, being customer-focused, understanding and meeting customer needs, coddling customers with Tender Loving Care, and giving quality customer service became a critical organizational goal—and received spotlight attention. Books were written. Banners hung. And speeches made. All trumpeting the importance of customer service. A revolution in the way customer service was viewed and valued began—and continues to this day.

In the half dozen years since the start of the latest service revolution, we've all learned a lot about what it takes to create and sustain a service advantage. And for all we've learned, for all that has been written and said, the most important part of creating a "service advantage"—is still you.

What you do is important. What you do is work—hard work. Answering questions. Solving problems. Untangling corporate log jams. Fixing what's broken and finding what's lost. Soothing the irate and reassuring the timid. And time after time, performing the business equivalent of pulling a rabbit out of a hat: Matching people with whom you do business with just the right products and services, and helping them enjoy and get the most out of those purchases.

The original *Delivering Knock Your Socks Off Service* was written to share with you what we had learned about quality customer care during fifteen years of watching and working with thousands of customer-oriented customer service professionals. People just like you who provide great service over and over and over again; true Knock Your Socks Off Service pros who make their customers' lives and jobs simpler instead of more difficult, more interesting and less boring— and who have a heck of a good time doing it.

In the ensuing ten-plus years we have had the opportunity to work with thousands of customer service professionals worldwide. And we have learned still more about the fine art of delivering world-class customer care. We have taken those lessons in hand and to heart and present here for your consideration the twenty-first century edition of *Delivering Knock Your Socks Off Service.*

Whether you are new to customer service or an old pro, we think there is something here for you. What you do is more important to your organization than ever before. If this book helps you to do it even a little bit better, thank the thousands of pros who taught us, not us. And if you find the journey through these pages not only helpful, but enjoyable, then we'll have met *our* customer service goal.

Ron Zemke

Our Thanks

There has never been and never will be a *Knock Your Socks Off Service* book that is the product of a single mind, set of hands, or isolated creative act—or that has written itself. All eight of the books and the various revisions and updates are the product of a team effort: sometimes the New York Yankees, occasionally the Keystone Kops, but a team effort nonetheless—and a fun one. That means there are a lot of thank-yous and kudos to pass around.

Performance Research Associates partners Chip Bell and Tom Connellan and Minneapolis lead trainer Ann Thomas contributed to the content of this edition through their encouragement and generous sharing of service insights from their work with clients and from laboring with the darnedest assortment of customer service issues one could imagine. There will never be enough Jack Daniels to repay the long hours they spent sharing stories and mining their experiences for this book's benefit.

Jill Applegate not only typed the manuscript over and over again, but inadvertently earned a working Ph.D. in project management. She's still the only one who knows where all of the pieces are.

John Bush continues to amaze us with his creative illustrations and his ability to combine whimsy with truth.

Ellen Kadin, our AMACOM acquisitions editor, once again exhibited stoic calm amid the swells of craziness and cotton candy deadlines we created. Hank Kennedy, AMACOM publisher, earned a lifetime exemption from bad thoughts about publishers for his unbelievable negotiation skills and the infinite patience he exhibited in navigating the last-minute obstacles that threatened to derail the project. Thanks Hank.

A very, very special thank you to Susan Zemke. The time and energy she spent challenging older concepts and surfacing contemporary issues for consideration in this edition is beyond repayment. All on top of her own demanding consulting schedule at the Minneapolis office of Linkage, Inc.

I

The Fundamental Principles of Knock Your Socks Off Service

Delivering Knock Your Socks Off Service—the kind of service that makes a positive, lasting impression on your customers—takes more than simple courtesy. Much more.

The first fundamental is understanding what good service is—from your customer's point of view. What you do, how you do it, knowing how well it must be done, and doing it again and again—those are fundamental as well.

Delivering Knock Your Socks Off Service means creating a positive, memorable experience for every customer. It means meeting expectations and satisfying needs—in such a way that you're seen as easy to do business with. It means looking for opportunities to wow and delight your customer in unique and unexpected ways.

The customer who experiences all that will be your customer again and again. When you deliver Knock Your Socks Off Service, everybody wins: Your customer, your company, and *you*.

1

1

The Only Unbreakable Rule:

To the Customer, *You* Are the Company

Customer relations is an integral part of your job—not an extension of it.

—William B. Martin

Quality Customer Service

Customers don't distinguish between you and the organization you work for. Nor should they. To your customer's way of thinking, you *are* the company.

Customers don't know how things get done behind doors marked "Employees Only." They don't know your areas of responsibility, your job description, or what you personally can and cannot do for them. And they don't care. To customers, those things are *your* business, not theirs.

Their attitude and focus is clear and straightforward: "Help me with this purchase, please." "Serve me my meal." "Solve my problem." "Process my order, *now*." Whether customers' feelings about the company are good or bad often relates directly to their experience with you and the way you help them meet their needs.

Each interaction between a customer and a service professional is one moment in the chain of the customer's experience. If you're a service person, and you get it wrong at your link in the chain, you are very likely erasing from the customer's mind all the memories of good treatment he or she may have had up to that moment. But if you get it right, you have a chance to undo all the wrongs that may have happened before the customer got to you.

Consider this small example from a trip to Walt Disney World—the land where service magic abounds! A friend of ours was there recently, enjoying a hot, summer day at the Magic Kingdom. After waiting in line for about 20 minutes for an ice cream cone, she started off down Main Street USA, licking intently. She glanced away for a second, and when she looked back, found herself staring dumbfounded at an empty cone! What had happened? An uninvited sea gull had swooped down and scooped the ice cream right out of the cone. She was stunned, but continued her walk down Main Street USA more than a little miffed at the situation. Seconds later, a young man carrying a broom and dust pan, approached her: "Excuse me, Ma'am, I saw that bird dive at your ice cream. Unfortunately, I see that fairly frequently. Disney's sea gulls pretty much know no fear. May I escort you back to get you another cone? That was cookies and cream, wasn't it?" Our friend was thunderstruck! What could have been a negative moment, turned full circle and is now a favorite Walt Disney World memory; one she loves to share with others.

Just like that Disney employee, you can make or break the chain of great service and memorable experiences. Is it fair that so much can depend on you? Nope. But fair has nothing to do with it.

When your job involves serving customers and dealing with the public, how good a job you do with and for them— for the nice and the nasty, the smart and the dumb, the people you'd like to take home to mother, and those you really wish had never been born—determines how successful your company will be. In short:

> You Are the Company

TIP: Use *I* instead of *they* or *we*. To a customer, the company begins and ends with you. Using *I* shows that you understand and accept that: "*I'm* sorry you had to look so long to find the dress department. May *I* help you find anything else?"

Being the Company: It's Everything You Do

Some of the things you do to provide Knock Your Socks Off Service are relatively simple and easy, such as choosing your language carefully.

Other actions you take are more complex. Customers expect you to make the organization work for them. They expect you to understand the big picture and to be able to answer

their questions, solve their problems, and refer them to just the right people for just the right things.

> **TIP:** Saying "the *policy* is. . . ." or "*they* won't allow. . . ." tells customers you are just a clerk. If that's the way you feel, you won't ever be able to help them—and could easily be replaced by a machine or walked on like so much carpet. Verbally separating yourself from the company in the customer's mind can take you off the hot seat with cross customers, but it plants a seed of doubt in the customer's mind. It says: "You may not be able to trust me to help you."

What your customers want and need is changing constantly. So is your company, and so are you. How can you possibly keep up? Let the following three questions guide your personal-service efforts. Don't just ask them once. Ask them all the time. Use the information they provide to choose actions that will Knock the Socks Off your customers.

1. *What do my customers want from me and from my company?* Think about what your customers *need* and what your customers *expect*. If you don't know—ask around. The seasoned senior associates will have a pretty good idea.

2. *How do support areas—e.g., billing or shipping—work to serve my customers?* Consider your role in helping the different areas of your company work in harmony for your customer. Who do you need in your corner to help you help your customers?

3. *What are the details—little things—that make a big difference in my customers' satisfaction?* Knock Your Socks Off Service means paying attention to what's important in your customers' eyes. Do you know what counts for your customers?

Being the company to your customers is what makes the work you do challenging and rewarding. In your one-to-one contact with customers, the once vague, impersonal company takes on shape and substance. The power to make that contact magical and memorable is in your hands. The power to keep customers coming back is in your hands.

From this moment forward, make this your pledge:

2

Know What Knock Your Socks Off Service Is

Customers perceive service in their own unique, idiosyncratic, emotional, irrational, end-of-the-day, and totally human terms. Perception is all there is!

—Tom Peters
Management Guru

Customers are demanding. And they have every right to be. Today's customers have more options and less time than ever before. If your organization doesn't offer what they want or need, if you don't interact with them in a manner that meets or exceeds their expectations, and you aren't quick about it, they will just walk on down the street—or let their fingers surf the `Net—and do business with one of your competitors.

And if you don't have customers, you don't have a job!

Researchers consistently find that it costs *five times more* to attract a new customer than it does to keep one you already have. But many businesses think only of making the sale instead of developing long-term customer relationships. Even more disturbing, researchers also find that at any given time, as many as *one customer in four* is dissatisfied enough to start doing business with someone else—if he or she can find someone else who promises to do the same thing that you do but in a slightly more satisfying way. That's as many as twenty-five out of every one hundred people your organization does business with. Most disturbing of all is the finding that *only one* of those twenty-five dissatisfied customers will ever tell you that he or she is dissatisfied. In fact, you've probably noticed from your own experience how rare it is to deal with customers who can do a really good job of telling you what they want. More often, they just expect you to know—and are disappointed when you don't.

That's why companies spend a lot of time and money these days observing customers as they shop, surveying them by mail, talking to them on the phone, and meeting them face-to-face. Like miners working a claim for the gold they know is there, today's businesses collect and sort customer letters and comment cards, looking for the complaints and the compliments that provide clues about what people want today—and how their needs may change tomorrow.

As a customer service professional, you frequently draw on the knowledge your company has acquired about customers. But you have another, equally important source of information: Your own day-to-day contact with your customers. From personal experience, you know quite a lot about what your customers want: Which actions meet their expectations, which exceed them—and which disappoint them.

That's your own special edge, the foundation on which to build your own unique way of providing Knock Your Socks Off Service.

Getting Yourself Organized: The RATER Factors

It's helpful to have a framework to hold together the things you know personally and the information passed on to you by your organization. The framework we like a lot was invented by Texas A&M researcher Dr. Leonard Berry and his colleagues at Texas A&M University. They have found that customers evaluate service quality on five factors:

1. *Reliability.* The ability to provide what was promised, dependably and accurately.
2. *Assurance.* The knowledge and courtesy you show to

customers, and your ability to convey trust, competence, and confidence.

3. *Tangibles.* The physical facilities and equipment, and your own (and others') appearance.
4. *Empathy.* The degree of caring and individual attention you show customers.
5. *Responsiveness.* The willingness to help customers promptly.

TIP: Combining the first letter of each factor **R**eliability, **A**ssurance, **T**angibles, **E**mpathy, **R**esponsiveness, spells the word RATER. It is a handy way to remember these important attributes. Try organizing what you know about clients using RATER. Example: In Mr. Smith's file, next to Responsiveness, you could have a note that reminds you of his responsiveness preferences. Something like "customer is sensitive to call backs. Return all his calls ASAP."

Chances are, almost everything you do to and for your customers falls into one of these categories. Consider these common examples:

- When you fulfill a customer order on time, you show *reliability.*
- When you smile and tell a customer, "I can help you with that"—and do—you build *assurance.*
- And when you take the time to make yourself and your work area presentable, you are paying attention to the *tangibles.*
- When you are sensitive to an individual customer's needs when solving a problem, you show *empathy.*
- When you notice a customer puzzling over a product and offer help and information, you show *responsiveness.*

All five factors are important to your customers. In the next five chapters, we will look at each of these pieces of the customer service puzzle in more detail to see how they combine to create people-pleasing Knock Your Socks Off Service.

Customer expectations of service organizations are loud and clear: look good, be responsive, be reassuring through courtesy and competence, be empathetic but, most of all, be reliable. Do what you said you would do. Keep the service promise.

—Dr. Leonard Berry
Researcher, Texas A&M University

3

Knock Your Socks Off Service Is:

Reliable

Undertake not what you cannot perform but be careful to keep your promise.

—George Washington

As commander-in-chief of the Continental forces in the American Revolution, George Washington was well aware that the lives of thousands of men and the fate of an emerging nation rested on his ability to know what could and could not be accomplished. He had to deliver on his commitments. There was no room for misjudging the situation.

As a service professional, you are part of another kind of revolution: the service revolution. And while lives are seldom on the line, a little piece of the future of your company is—every time you face a customer. That's where reliability comes in.

The Service Promise

Reliability means keeping the Service Promise—doing what you say you will do for the customer. To the customer, the Service Promise has three distinct parts: organizational commitments, common expectations, and personal promises.

12

• *Organizational commitments.* Organizations make direct promises to customers through advertising and marketing materials, in company correspondence and contracts, and in service guarantees and policies published for everyone to see. In addition to these, customers will hold the company to indirect commitments—promises that customers believe are implied in the way the company talks about itself, its products, and its services. Or customers may hold organizations to commitments that they believe are "standard" for the industry.

Consider customer expectations about overnight delivery services. FedEx Corporation, an international overnight delivery service, promises and provides moment-by-moment package tracing. If you want to confirm that your package will arrive on time, simply tap into FedEx's computer tracking system to learn that your package is in a truck on the corner of Maple and Vine, and expected to reach its destination within 15 minutes. Other shippers should not be surprised when customers demand, "What do you mean you can't tell me exactly where my package is? You're in the overnight shipping business so you have to be able to do that!" Fair or not, FedEx set a standard others are being held to, what standards has your competition set for you?

• *Common expectations.* Your customers bring additional expectations with them to every service transaction. Based on their past experiences with you and with other service providers, customers make assumptions about what you can and can't do for them. Failing to meet a customer expectation, whether you knew about it or not—even whether you helped to shape it or not—has the same impact as breaking any other promise.

For example, many restaurants routinely post a sign warning that they "cannot be responsible for items left in the cloak room." However, when customers hand their items di-

rectly to an attendant, most assume that the belongings will be
guarded. Having a staffed coat check rather than an isolated
coat rack creates an expectation of security, even if there is a
clear warning to the contrary.

> • *Personal promises.* The majority of customer service
> promises come from you. These are the promises you
> make when you tell a customer, "I'll get right back to
> you with that information," or "You should expect to
> receive that package in two weeks," or "I understand
> the problem you are having with your computer, and
> this software support download will solve it." You are
> underwriting those promises.

Knowing what your customers expect is the first step to
creating Knock Your Socks Off Service. By asking questions of
your customers and your colleagues, and really listening,
you'll be able to discover the details of the Service Promise
your customers expect you to fulfill.

Managing Promises

The Service Promise can and should be managed. Once you
know what your customers do and don't expect—the promise
they want you to make—you are in a position to shape your
customers' expectations to match what you actually can and
will do for them. When you do that well, customers judge you
and your organization to be reliable.

Let's say you are a salesperson in a store selling custom-
built furniture. Jane Dowe comes in looking for a desk and cre-
denza. She's never purchased custom-built furniture before,
and assumes (has an expectation) that you have most models
in stock and that she'll be able to take her purchase home with
her today. Your challenge is to change her expectations to
match what your organization can do for her.

You show your organization's promise—commitment to
quality products—by leading her to several sample desks and
credenzas on the showroom floor. Perhaps there is even a display showing the custom manufacturing process. You rein-

force the organization's message with a personal promise: "Our custom desks allow us to combine the features that best meet your needs with the highest quality craftsmanship. If we can finalize the design today, I can have your desk delivered in two weeks."

Now Jane has a clear understanding of the Service Promise. She may decide that the wait is worth it because of the quality involved. If she really needs the desk today, in which case you can't change her expectations *this* time, at least she will leave your store knowing the difference between custom-made and off-the-shelf, and knowing that you are concerned with her satisfaction. And she may recommend you to a friend or colleague based on her revised understanding of your capabilities.

Fixing Promises When They Break

Sometimes promises made in good faith can't be kept. As much as we strive to be error-free, it's inevitable that problems will occur. Not everything that affects your customer's experience with you is within your control. What should you do when the Service Promise is broken? When you discover a broken promise or have one pointed out to you, the first thing to do is to apologize. Don't waste time scapegoating—blaming yourself, your company, or your customer. Admit that something has gone wrong, and immediately find out what your customer needs now. Has the broken promise created another problem? Or has it, perhaps, created an opportunity for you to rescue your reputation for reliability?

> **TIP:** Never overpromise just to get the sale. In today's service-sensitive economy, service doesn't end with the sale, it just begins. Keeping the promises you make and only making promises you can keep is what reliability is all about.

For example, suppose Jane Dowe, the desk buyer, understands that her delivery will take two weeks, but you've just found out that deliveries are running about three days behind schedule. If you don't call with the bad news, you can bet she'll call you when the desk doesn't arrive on the day she was told to expect it—and she won't be happy about the delay.

However, if you take the initiative, you might discover that the delay is acceptable. Or, if she has an important meeting and needs furniture in her office on that specific day, you can arrange for a loaner until the order arrives. Then, you (and your company) look like a hero.

> You can't promise your customers sunny weather, but you can promise to hold an umbrella over them when it rains.
>
> —Sign in a telephone service center

4

Knock Your Socks Off Service Is:

Responsive

A rose on time is far more valuable than a $1,000 gift that's too late.

—Jim Rohn
Author and motivational speaker

Timeliness has always been important. And today, responsive action—doing things in a timely fashion—is even more crucial. Just look around at the number of businesses that have been created to get things done quickly:

- FedEx won international success by delivering letters and small parcels "Absolutely, Positively, Anytime."
- LensCrafters optical stores promise "Custom-Crafted Eyeglasses in About an Hour."
- Amazon.com guarantees that every transaction you make will be safe.
- Lands' End vows that all in-stock orders leave the distribution center—the size of sixteen football fields—the next business day after they're ordered. Standard delivery (no surcharge) is two business days to every state but Hawaii and Alaska.

The big-name national service leaders don't have a corner on the timeliness market. All over town, you can find same-day dry cleaning, fifty-five-minute photo developing, and twenty-four-hour automated banking services. At the same time, a growing number of traditional manufacturing companies are practicing Just-In-Time (JIT) management, ordering things to arrive just in time. Sometimes "just in the nick of time."

Companies that cater to time conscious customers are everywhere you look. Their success affects your customers' expectations of your willingness and ability to do the same. Small wonder that your customers may be demanding tighter deadlines and faster service than ever before. When they see others promising fast, fast, fast, they expect the same from you.

Setting—and Meeting—Deadlines

Sometimes it seems that everybody wants everything done at the same time. But it's a mistake to automatically think your customers won't accept anything less than "right this instant." On the other hand, giving yourself too much extra "wiggle room," time to do the work, can make you look slow, and leave you and your company looking unresponsive.

Start by finding out what the customer really needs by when. There's a big difference between, "I have to have this dry-cleaned to wear next week," and "I want to have these winter coats cleaned before I put them away for the season." Use that information to pick a time that works well for you and try it out on the customer. Nine times out of ten, you'll hear "yes." If your suggestion doesn't work, your customer will let you know and you can work together to find an alternative. Customers appreciate and remember such responsiveness to their needs.

TIP: The next time you're in doubt, ask your customers, "When would you like this?" You may be pleasantly surprised when they pick a reasonable time, or even ask you: "Well, when could you have it done?" An added benefit is that it gives them a sense of control and involvement. We are all more comfortable when we feel we have some control over our lives and the things that go on around us.

Deadlines are important. But deadlines are created by people. When you say to a customer, "I'll have it ready for you this afternoon," or "I'll put it in the mail today," you are creating an expectation for your customer and setting a deadline for yourself. Be realistic, because once created, deadlines become yardsticks by which your customer will measure your success or failure. Knock Your Socks Off Service results from creating acceptable, realistic expectations of responsiveness in your customers' minds, and then meeting those expectations.

When Customers Must Wait

The best time for anything is the time that is best for the customer. But dissatisfaction isn't always measured in minutes. Rather, dissatisfaction is often the result of uncertainty. Research shows that the most frustrating aspect of waiting is *not knowing how long the wait will be.*

Be aware of what your customers think is an acceptable wait. According to a study by *Restaurants & Institutions* magazine, for example, "fast" for fast-food customers means five minutes or less, while diners in a family restaurant are willing to wait as long as thirty minutes for their specially prepared food to arrive. Similarly, in the retail business, expectations may vary with the time of day or season of the year. Customers are less able, let alone less willing, to wait around for help during their lunch hour than on a lazy Sunday afternoon, and certainly the holiday shopping season has its own pace compared to other times of the year.

Think about your own experiences as a customer. When you are in line behind someone who insists on paying off the national debt in pennies or are waiting for the manufacturer to plant and grow the oak trees to make your new furniture, it is the uncertainty: "Will I be served sometime this century?" more than the wait itself that gets your blood pumping. As a service professional, you may not be able to count pennies any faster or make trees grow overnight, but you can make waiting less traumatic. Acknowledge waiting customers and keep them informed about what is happening. Be as specific as you can: "I'm with another customer right now, but should be free in about fifteen minutes. If you would like to look around some more, I'll come find you the minute I'm through."

> **TIP:** Pay special attention to waiting time when your customers are out of your sight, whether on the phone, in another part of town, or in another state, rather than standing right in front of you. Out of sight is much more worrisome to customers.

In face-to-face settings, acknowledgment doesn't have to be verbal. In the words of one restaurateur, "Make eye contact with the customers. Make your actions say, 'I know you are there. I'll be with you very soon.'"

> Our customer support is so responsive that, Oops, there's a call, gotta go!
>
> —Mind Spring Internet Service advertisement

5

Knock Your Socks Off Service Is:

Reassuring

Consistent, high-quality service boils down to two
equally important things: caring and competence.

—Chip R. Bell and Ron Zemke
Service Wisdom

In many companies, the desire to improve service quality has
given birth to countless hours of "smile training," as though
the key to satisfying every customer's needs and expectations
involved nothing more than a cheery greeting and a happy-
face sticker. Today's customer service professionals know
there's much more involved in creating customer satisfaction
than smiles and happy faces.

If being nice were the complete answer, good service
would be the norm, but that's clearly not the case. Make no
mistake: Courtesy, good manners, and civility are important—
treat your customers like dirt and they'll make your life mis-
erable every time. But courtesy is not a substitute for competence and skill.

When you provide Knock Your Socks Off Service, your
actions assure customers that they are doing business with a
well-trained, skillful service professional. Customers know

they can trust you because of the competence and confidence you display in your work.

Today, customers expect to be reassured—to be made to feel comfortable—by the people they deal with. And that takes more than mastery of a few simple "people skills." It's the combination of style and substance that wins accolades and brings customers back again and again.

Bad Service Drives Customers Away

Knock Your Socks Off Service professionals know that inept service has profound consequences. One study on retailing reports that customers identify "salespeople who know less about their products than I do" as a leading reason for switching from department store to catalog shopping. Another study finds that two out of three car buyers refuse to return to the same dealership for their next car. Their reasons for doing so have little to do with the car itself and more to do with the games on the showroom floor and the boorish treatment they encountered when they brought the family chariot in for service that made them determined to look elsewhere. Today the number of potential customers that know more about your products than you do is higher than ever before. According to Chip Horner, vice president of Pfizer Consumer Group in Morris Plains, New Jersey, "Customers have done a lot more research, they go to the web, and they save the toughest choice questions for the phone call or the e-mail to our call centers. Some of those questions are so obscure that we have to be prepared for the unexpected in much more detail."

This is why providing Knock Your Socks Off Service has such a positive impact on your company, your customer, and your career. Good service providers stand out, so make yourself memorable. Combine substance and style—what you do and how you do it—to reassure your customers that you really do know, and care about, what you are doing.

The Reassurance Factor

The reassurance factor is about managing your customers' feelings of trust. The customer's decision to trust you is built on honesty, knowledge, and know-how. It is the substance that backs up your style, and it comes in four packages:

1. *Product knowledge.* Customers expect you to know the features, advantages, and benefits of whatever it is your company makes, does, or delivers. The salesperson who has to read the manual in front of the customer to figure out how to turn on the stereo doesn't create an impression of competence.

2. *Company knowledge.* Customers expect you to know more than the limits of your particular job. They expect you to know how your organization works so you can guide them to someone who can meet their needs if those needs should fall outside your area of responsibility. Can you help your customer navigate the briar patch that is your business easily and successfully?

3. *Listening skills.* Customers expect you to listen, understand, and respond to their specific needs as they explain them to you. They expect you to ask pertinent questions that help them do a better job of giving you the information you need to work for them effectively. And they expect you to pay attention and get it right so they don't have to repeat it. And they expect you to tell the truth when a thing can't be done or done in the time frame they want.

4. *Problem-solving skills.* Customers expect that you will be able to recognize their needs as they express them and be

able to quickly align them with the services your organization provides. When things go wrong or don't work, they expect you to know how to fix things—and fix them fast.

Extra Points for Style

A competent annual physical performed by a rude, disheveled, or distracted physician isn't likely to be a satisfying experience for the patient, regardless of the technical excellence of the doctor. Once you've mastered the fundamentals of competence, it's your confident style that sets you apart. It starts with first impressions. In their book, *Contact: The First Four Minutes* (Ballantine Books, 1994), Leonard and Natalie Zunin contend that "the first four minutes of any contact is a kind of audition." In some customer service situations, you may have far less time than that—many transactions today are over in twenty to sixty seconds.

But first impressions are only the beginning. In service, everything communicates your style to customers. The way you dress, the way you move, or whether you move at all instead of staying barricaded behind a desk or cash register. The way you talk; your e-mail greeting; the way you do or don't make eye contact, listen, and respond. The way you act when you're not taking care of customers, but are still within their view. The way you take care of the person ahead of them in line. All these impressions add up to say, "I know what you need. I can take care of that for you."

Reliable service, delivered quickly and confidently, by knowledgeable, courteous people—what more could your customers want?

> I always wanted to fully understand the situation before I made a commitment. It finally dawned on me that my customer needs the reassurance of my commitment, before he'll give me time to understand the problem.
>
> —Customer Service Representative
>   SemiConductor Manufacturing Company

6

Knock Your Socks Off Service Is:

Empathetic

The more high tech the world becomes, the more people crave high-touch service.

—John Naisbett
Megatrends

Customers come in a wide variety of shapes and sizes, and they bring an equally wide variety of wants, needs, expectations, attitudes, and emotions with them to the service transaction. Consequently, customers want to be treated as individuals. No one likes to be treated like a number by a service worker responding like a machine. Recognizing your customers' emotional states helps you figure out the best way to effectively and professionally serve them.

Consider how you might treat these two customers if you were the banquet manager for a fancy hotel:

- Tom Timid walks into the catering office looking nervous and tense. He is planning a special retirement party for his boss of ten years and he's obviously never organized a function like this before.

- Demanding Doris is an old hand at hosting special events. The annual sales department gala will be the fourth major event she has organized this year. When she walks into the banquet office, Doris knows exactly what she wants. Her you-all-just-stand-back-and-take-orders attitude is clearly visible.

How do you treat Tom and Doris as individuals? For Tom, it is important to make him comfortable and take the time to make him "feel smart" about the event planning process and supported by you:

> "Tom, you can depend on me to be there every step of the way. To begin with, why don't you tell me a little bit more about your event, and then I'll show you our step-by-step planning process."

The same technique would probably frustrate, possibly even anger, Doris. She may see your friendly, in-depth explanation as a waste of her valuable time. She expects you to credit her with the savvy she has shown on previous occasions:

> "Hello, Doris. It's good to work with you again. I see you brought an outline of everything you need. You

always make my job so much easier! Let me take a look and see if I have any questions."

Seeing—and treating—each customer as an individual helps you meet the needs of each on their own unique level.

Empathy vs. Sympathy

Whatever the emotional state of your customers—cautious or confident—it's important to each of them that you understand what they're trying to tell you and how they feel about the services they want you to provide. But when emotions run high, especially when things are going wrong, it's easy to get caught up in a customer's emotional world.

When responding to customers' emotions, it's helpful to make a distinction between empathy and sympathy. Both have to do with how you respond to other people's emotions. Many people use the terms interchangeably, but the difference is real and important.

- *Sympathy* involves identifying with, and even taking on, another person's emotions. A sympathetic response is, "I'm really angry about those centerpieces, too."
- *Empathy* means acknowledging and affirming another's emotional state. An empathetic response is, "I can understand why that makes you angry."

TIP: When a service provider wallows in a customer's misfortune, there are two victims instead of one. As a service professional, you need to see the clear difference between what happened and who it happened to—and work on the former to bring things back to normal.

What's the Difference?

Responding to customers with sympathy—getting as upset as they are—puts you on an emotional roller coaster and can leave you worn out and frazzled at the end of the day. The trick is to be emotionally aware and sensitive without becoming too emotionally involved. When you respond with empathy, you stay calm and in control of yourself. Only then are you at your absolute best: ready, willing, and able to help your customer meet his needs or solve his problem.

Showing empathy for customers allows you to be professional and caring at the same time. It also makes customers feel like important individuals. Empathy cannot be handed out by a machine; it's something one person does for another. There is no substitute for the human touch you provide when you deliver Knock Your Socks Off Service. That's what makes high-quality service such hard work. It's also what makes it so rewarding.

> Customers don't care what you know, until they know that you care.
>
> —Digital Equipment Corp.
> Customer Service Department

7

Knock Your Socks Off Service Is:

Tangibles

From the customer's point of view, if they can see it, walk on it, hold it, hear it, step in it, smell it, carry it, step over it, touch it, use it, even taste it, if they can feel it or sense it, it's customer service.

—SuperAmerica Training Program

Service is difficult to describe in tangible, physical terms. It's fuzzy. Mushy. Slippery. You can't bottle a trip to the movies or an appendectomy any more than you can put a yardstick to advice from a stockbroker or ideas from an interior decorator. Twenty minutes with a physician or auto mechanic isn't necessarily better or worse than ten minutes or thirty minutes. It's the quality of what is accomplished, not the quantity of the time involved. One of the major complications in providing service comes from the fact that so much of it is intangible.

Yet in every service encounter, there are tangibles before, during, and after the fact that affect the way customers judge the quality of the service you're providing. If you work in a hotel and a customer asks you for directions to an off-property restaurant and you point the way, that's intangible. Drawing a map is a way to make the service tangible. Having a preprinted map and specific directions is both tangible and Knock your Socks Off Service! The fifth and final key to mastering the fundamentals of Knock Your Socks Off Service is understanding the role tangibles play in making your intangible service memorable and satisfying.

Think about going out to eat:

- *Before* you enter a restaurant, you evaluate it based on some of its tangible attributes: the advertising you've seen or heard, the location as you drive up, and the cleanliness of the parking lot where you leave your car. Can you smell the aroma of good food or the remains of half-eaten meals rotting in the dumpster? Do the building and grounds look well-kept? Is the sign lit and legible?
- *As you walk through the front door,* you make more judgments. Does the host or hostess look friendly? Does the establishment appear to be clean? (And if it's not, do you really want to eat the food?) Is there a place to hang or check your coat? Can you find the restrooms or the telephone without a guide?
- *During* your meal, you evaluate other tangibles, from standard expectations about the menu and the tableware to unique items such as the special hat you see a waitress give a small child or the balloons passed out to a group celebrating a birthday. You judge the way your food is presented—how it looks on the plate and how closely it resembles the wonderful picture you saw on the menu—as well as how it tastes.
- *Afterward,* there are more forms of tangible evidence for you to weigh. When the bill arrives, is it clean, accurate, and clearly understandable, or do you get the impression that it absorbed more of your meal than you did? If you use the restroom, is it clean? If you paid your $19.01 bill with a twenty dollar bill, did your server bring you ninety-nine cents in change, or a crisp, new single?

Demonstrating Value

Tangibles help convey the value of the service transaction's intangible aspects. They're an important way for you to educate your customers and help them evaluate the quality of service you've provided. Manage the tangible aspects of the encounter and you give your customers something solid to tie their impressions to.

> **TIP:** If you're helping a customer estimate the cost of a purchase, be it a new stereo system or a roomful of carpet, write your calculations neatly on a page with your name, phone number, and e-mail address. Your customer will appreciate having it as a reference and will easily remember who provided such terrific service.

The best rule of thumb regarding the tangibles you manage is: Never give something to customers you'd be reluctant, embarrassed, or angered to receive yourself. Here are three ways you can demonstrate the value of the service transaction:

1. Take pride in your own appearance and the look and feel of the materials you give to your customers. Hand them

over personally instead of tossing them on a countertop or leaving it to the customers to figure out what to gather up and how to organize and carry them. Treat your materials with respect and your customers will respect, and remember positively, what you have done for them.

2. When customers give you their name, phone number, or other information, write it down. This demonstrates that you think the information is important. And make a point of getting it right—read it back to make sure there's no mistake. Today, people are nervous about who has their personal information. Be sure they see you safeguarding it.

3. Make sure the parts of your workplace customers see—and especially those they touch—are clean, safe, and as comfortable as you can make them.

When your customers describe your service to their friends and colleagues—people who could become your next customers—they will focus on their observations of tangible things. To keep customers coming back again and again, you want those tangibles to reflect well on you and the service you provide.

First impressions are the most lasting.

—Proverb

8

Customers Are Everywhere—Inside and Out

Who does my work go to?
Who Is my work important to?

—Dun & Bradstreet

At Dun & Bradstreet, the giant data management and research company, every employee is required to answer those two questions in order to identify their customers, no matter where on the organizational ladder they may be.

Dun & Bradstreet recognizes that great service doesn't just happen on the front line, where service providers come face to face with customers as consumers. The fact that you may never see the customers who ultimately buy and use the products and services your company provides doesn't make you any less of a service professional. Not on your life. Everyone has a customer, just as everyone is a customer.

There are two basic types of customers

1. *External customers.* The people who buy your products and services. They are external to, or outside of, your company; they are the source of the revenue that funds continuing operations. Without them, you won't be in business for very long.

2. *Internal customers.* These are your associates, other people who work for your organization. Regardless of whether they are at another location in your building, in another state or country, or sitting at the next desk in your department, if they depend on you and the work you do to complete their own work—often so they can serve their own customers—*they* are your customers.

There's a remarkably close and consistent link between how internal customers are treated and how external customers perceive the quality of your organization's services. Benjamin Schneider, professor of psychology and business management at the University of Maryland, is well known for his research on how "the people make the place." He notes that a commitment to serve internal customers invariably shows itself to external customers, and that it's almost impossible to provide good external service if your organization is not providing good internal service. Without a commitment to high-quality, Knock Your Socks Off Service inside an organization, service to end-user consumers will surely suffer.

Identifying Your Customers

Several years ago a man named Jan Carlzon led a remarkable turnaround that brought his company, Scandinavian Airlines System (SAS) from an $8 million loss to a gross profit of $71 million in less than two years. He didn't resort to new advertising or clever accounting gimmicks. He did it by inspiring an uncompromising focus on the customer at every level of the airline. Part of that focus involved changing the way people within the airline interacted with each other.

Carlzon's hope was to make SAS the best possible air travel choice for business travelers. To do that, he believed that every employee of the airline had to focus on customer service. But Carlzon knew that not everyone in the company had direct interaction with external customers—the passengers boarding the planes. In fact, a very significant portion of SAS employees served only internal customers.

- Maintenance workers made it possible for ground crews and pilots to keep the planes flying on time.
- Catering staff kept the planes well stocked with food and beverages so flight attendants could keep passengers fed and comfortable.
- And managers had to do whatever it took to serve their front line people so that they, in turn, could serve passengers.

To make sure everyone knew where they stood in the new SAS, Carlzon proclaimed a simple, universal job description: "If you're not serving the customer, your job is to be serving someone who is." That told everyone, from front-line personnel to management, that the airline could only survive if they all worked together to make the organization function on their passengers' behalf. It also told everyone where to focus their efforts: on service.

Internal Customers

External customers are pretty easy to identify. However, sometimes it's difficult to identify your customers when they are inside your organization. Maybe you don't see them face to face.

Maybe you're not sure what happens to your work when it leaves your desk or department. Maybe the same people you serve also serve you. The customer/service provider relationship within an organization is not static. It can change from day to day, from moment to moment.

> **TIP:** In your organization, your customer is whoever benefits from the work you do—or, conversely, whoever suffers when your work is done poorly or not at all. Think about a time when you had an unavoidable and unexpected absence from work. Who on your work team was affected? That person or those people are your internal customers.

If, for example, you take customer orders at your company's telephone center, obviously you are serving external customers directly. But you have internal customers, too. Who receives the orders you take from those external customers? What happens when necessary information is missing from those orders or is entered incorrectly? The impact of what you do or don't do affects your external customers, who may not receive what they ordered, and your internal customers in the warehouse, billing, and shipping who will have to deal with the complaint that comes when the order isn't received.

> **TIP:** Once you've identified your customers, talk to them about what they do and don't like about the service you provide for them. Use their feedback to improve the quality of the work you do.

Customers truly are everywhere, outside your organization as well as within. It is your job to identify your customers, know what they need from you, and how you can provide it for them. Doing so in ways that maximize both internal and external customer satisfaction is what creates that sense of teamwork and camaraderie that good organizations thrive on.

> If you're not serving the customer, your job is to be serving someone who is.
>
> —Jan Carlzon

9

The Ten Deadly Sins of Customer Service

Would *you* do business with you?
—Linda Silverman Goldzimer
"I'm First": Your Customer's Message to You

Everyone has pet peeves. Little things that annoy them beyond reason. When you were young, doing the obnoxious little things that set off your little brother or sister was fun—and funny. As adults, we recognize that annoying little habits and idiosyncratic behaviors are not only bad manners, they also can get you into serious trouble—especially on the job.

Knock Your Socks Off Service is a positive, reaching out philosophy. But part of serving well is knowing what *not* to do. It's impossible to anticipate everything that might get under the skin of a particular customer. But there are things that irritate almost all of us when we're on the customer side of the counter. Avoid these irritants for your own sake as well as your customers'.

Here are ten "sins" you can control—behaviors and actions that some service providers (never you or us!) exhibit that customers say annoy them most. While our list is based largely on our research with customers and service professionals, as well as on our own experience as customers, we're also indebted to Dr. Karl Albrecht's book, *At America's Service* (Business One Irwin, 1988).

Ten Sins You Can Control

1. *"I don't know."* A survey of retail customers in Washington, D.C., found the number one reason for switching to catalog or Internet shopping was that salespeople in stores were so ignorant about the merchandise. Customers expect you to know something about the products and services you sell. If you really can't answer a customer's question, instead of saying, "I don't know,"adding four essential words to the sentence—"but I'll find out" will make a huge difference.

2. *"I don't care."* Customers want you to care about serving them. They want to sense that you take pride in what you're doing. This reinforces that they've made a good choice by doing business with you. When your attitude, conversation, or appearance makes it clear you'd rather be somewhere else, they'll find themselves wishing the same thing.

3. *"I can't be bothered."* Actions really do speak louder than words. Believe it. If your conversation with a co-worker or an obviously personal phone call takes precedence over a customer, or you studiously ignore someone's attempt to catch your attention, your customers will be annoyed—and rightfully so.

4. *"I don't like you."* Customers are sensitive to attitudes that subtly or overtly say, "You're a nuisance; please go away." And no one enjoys the occasional encounter with a customer service person who is openly (or even covertly) hostile. The more aggressively obnoxious your behavior, the more memorable it will be for your customer, for all the wrong reasons.

5. *"I know it all."* When you jump in with a solution or comment before a customer has finished explaining his or her problem or question, that's being pushy. So, too, is trying to force a customer to make a buying decision. Knowledge is a tool to help you serve customers better, not a bludgeon with which to beat them into submission.

6. *"You don't know anything."* There are no dumb questions, only dumb answers. When you rudely or insensitively cut off, put down, or demean customers for having a confused or wrong idea of what exactly they need or what you can do for them, you slam the door in their face. Next time, they'll look for another door to walk their business through.

7. *"We don't want your kind here."* Prejudice, like customers, comes in all shapes, sizes, ages, colors, ethnicities, educational levels, and any other characteristic you care to name. But regardless of class or category, every customer is an individual who wants (and deserves) to be treated with courtesy and respect. Do you treat customers who show up in a suit and tie better than those who dress in jeans and a T-shirt? Do you assume that elderly customers won't be able to understand complex issues or that younger customers aren't seriously interested in buying anything? Your attitudes show in ways you may never even suspect.

8. *"Don't come back."* The purpose of serving customers well is to convince them to come back again and again. The easiest way to discourage that is to make it clear in words or actions that they're an inconvenience in your day that you'd just as soon be rid of once and for all. Thanking customers for their patronage and loyalty builds a relationship that can grow and mature.

9. *"I'm right and you're wrong."* One of the easiest (and most human) traps to fall into is arguing with a customer over

something that really is more a point of personal pride or pique than professional service. Customers are not always right, of course, but it doesn't cost you anything to give them the benefit of the doubt.

10. *"Hurry up and wait."* More than any other variable, *time*, and the lack of it, is the number one obsession for people today. Everyone starts with only twenty-four hours a day; no one wants to waste a minute of it, whether waiting for something to take place or being forced into a hasty decision that they'll sooner or later come to regret. Respect your customer's time and you'll find they respect you in return.

Baber's Rules of Customer Service

- Make the customers feel heard.
- Make the customers feel understood.
- Make the customers feel liked.
- Make the customers feel respected.
- Make the customers feel helped.
- Make the customers feel appreciated and respected.

—Michael Baber
Integrated Business Leadership Through Cross Marketing

10

The Customer Is Always . . .

The Customer

Our Policy
Rule 1: The customer is always right!
Rule 2: If the customer is ever wrong, reread Rule 1.
—Stew Leonard's Dairy Store
Norwalk, Connecticut

These words, chiseled into a 6,000-pound rock resting just outside the front door of Stew Leonard's, the world's largest (and most profitable) dairy store, are probably familiar.

They are also wrong.

So why do the people who run Stew Leonard's Dairy so loudly proclaim "Rule 1" and "Rule 2" at the entrance to the store? Because each and every employee knows, lives, and breathes the real truth behind the slogan written on the rock: Customers are not always right, but they are *always* our customers.

Right and Wrong

The customer is not always right. You know it. We know it. In fact, studies conducted by Arlington, Virginia-based TARP, a premier service research firm, even prove it scientifically. TARP finds that customers cause about a third of the service and product problems they complain about. Blindly believing or acting as if you believe the customer is always right, can be detrimental to you and to your customer.

Caution: Customers-are-always-right thinking can put a stop to problem solving and customer education. You can't correct a problem or a customer's misconception if you can't admit that it exists. Many times when customers cause problems—or believe untrue things—it's because we haven't taught them any differently. We are so familiar with the products we sell, and the services we supply that we forget how much there is to know, how much we have to help our customers learn.

Perhaps more dangerous is that customers-are-always-right thinking puts service providers in a one-down position. It says: "You're not paid to think or ask questions. Just smile and do whatever the customer tells you to do." No wonder that in such settings, service begins to feel like servitude: "Hello, my name is Pat and I'll be your personal slave this evening," is a bad mind-set.

Finally, blindly holding to the idea that customers are always right means that when something goes wrong—as it will, sooner or later—*you* must be wrong. You know that's not true. If you're behind the counter in a McDonald's and a customer walks up and orders McLobster and a bottle of McChampagne, it's very clear who's right and who's wrong. It's also irrelevant. Your job is to manage the encounter so the customer continues to be a customer. As in, "We're McOut of those two items but we have some other great things to eat here on our menu board."

Why We're There

The customer is our only reason for being there. Knowing that the customer is always the customer (not the problem, the enemy, or the bane of your existence) helps focus your effort where it belongs—on keeping the customer. The goal of every service transaction is, and must be, to satisfy and delight customers in ways that will keep them coming back for more.

As a service professional, you hold the power to make that happen. To do it, you need to be and act smart. You need to know more than your customer does about the products and services you sell and supply. You need to be sensitive to the fact that customers, like service professionals, are only human, with human faults and feelings. When customers are wrong, your role is to use your skills to help make them right, in a manner that neither embarrasses nor blames.

Three Ways to Make Customers Right

1. *Assume innocence.* "Guilty until proven innocent" doesn't play well with customers. Just because what they are saying sounds wrong to you, don't assume that it is. It may be that they are simply explaining what they need or want poorly, or that the directions they should have received were missing or misleading. Choose your words carefully:

> "I see what happened. This disc is a CD-R, not a CD-RW. Information can only be saved to it once, not over and over. Here's what we can do. . . "

2. *Look for teaching opportunities.* What information could your customers have used before the misunderstanding occurred? Make sure they get it now.

> "I'm glad you brought this to my attention. The information you needed was here in your packet, but I can see how it would be easy to miss, buried under so many other papers. Let's review your packet to see if I can head off any other surprises."

Or

> "I'm sorry you aren't happy with your Pez™ dispenser, but the head is supposed to go back like

that—that's how the candy is dispensed. I would be happy to refund your money, if that's what you'd like."

TIP: You can't educate the irate. When they are stressed and angry, customers do not take kindly to reeducation—"You know, you could have avoided all of this if you'd just remembered to...." Choosing to educate at the wrong moment is a sure way to add to the customer's upset. Look for ways to avoid embarrassing the customer when they have made a mistake or misunderstand something.

3. *Believe your customer.* Sometimes, the customer you initially think is 100 percent wrong will turn out to be right— or at least partly right—after all. The customer might, for instance, just be explaining the problem or complaint to you poorly. If you've ridden roughshod over the request or complaint, you're going to find yourself wolfing down a heaping helping of Humble Pie. The point of Knock Your Socks Off Service is to keep customer relationships intact. When in doubt, give your customer the benefit of the doubt.

"Let's check the advertising flyer to verify that the price you saw is for this model. Sure enough, there it is. Thanks for pointing that out to me. I'll make sure we get the shelf tags corrected so everyone knows which model is on sale."

Unfair Advantage

What about customers who try to use your service standards against you and get something for nothing, or a better deal than they are entitled to? First, it's important to recognize that truly dishonest customers are pretty rare. But they do exist.

Much more common are customers who honestly disagree with you about what is true and what is fair.

How do you tell the difference between legitimate and deceitful customer actions? We recommend the "Three Strikes and You're Out" policy used by Stuart Skorman, president of Empire Video of Keene, New Hampshire. The first time a customer and clerk disagree on whether a video was returned on time, "it must have been our mistake," Skorman says. Same thing the second time. But three strikes, and the customer's credibility is gone, the late charge stands.

> **NOTE:** Making a wrong customer right, without giving away the store, can be an incredible challenge. In fact, we wrote an entire book about it—*Knock Your Socks Off Answers: Solving Customer Nightmares and Soothing Nightmare Customers*(AMACOM, 1995), It's a great desk reference for figuring out tactful responses to customers.

Don't fix the blame. Fix the problem.
                                                            —Japanese saying

II

The How To's of Knock Your Socks Off Service

Outstanding customer service is a tapestry of individual actions that are important in the customer's eyes. Most are relatively easy and simple to master. Combined together, they make the service you provide truly memorable.

How well you listen, understand, and respond to each customer, how you handle face-to-face contact, how you use the telephone, the words you put on paper, the way you anticipate a customer's needs, and whether you thank them for doing business with you, all contribute to your customer's evaluation of your efforts.

Properly combined and skillfully executed, these elements add up to outstanding service, the kind that says, "I'm gonna knock your socks off!"

11

Honesty Is the Only Policy

A man always has two reasons for doing anything—a good reason, and the real reason.

—J. P. Morgan
Financier

When it comes to customer service, honesty isn't the best policy, it is the only policy. Lying to or misleading customers invariably leads to far worse problems than looking them straight in the eye and telling them something unpleasant they need to hear right now.

There are two very good reasons for facing your customer with the bad news.

First, tall tales inevitably catch up with you, and often in the most unexpected ways. Our partner, Tom Connellan, tells the story of a shipping clerk (let's call him Ralph) in a company in Michigan who had discovered a cute and, to his way of thinking, foolproof way of keeping customers off his back. Every morning he would bring three newspapers to work: the *New York Daily News*, the *Chicago Tribune,* and the *Los Angeles Times.* He would scan each carefully and circle any news item having to do with a transportation disaster—train wrecks and derailments, heavy snowfall in the Rocky Mountains, trucking strikes in the Southeast. You get the picture.

Then, for the rest of the day, any time a customer called up complaining that a promised shipment had not yet arrived, Ralph would put the caller on hold, thumb through the newspapers until he found a likely item, go back to the caller and ask: "Did you hear about the train that derailed outside Fort Worth last night? No? Well, it happened, and I know for a fact that your shipment was on that train. I'd like to help you out, but there's not a thing I can do about a natural disaster."

Ralph's little trick worked well for all of a year—until a customer, suspicious of the fact that three of his last five promised shipments were subject to "natural disasters," began checking around. To make a long story short, he figured out what Ralph was up to, put Ralph's company on his "Unreliable Vendor" list, and wrote a stinging letter to the president of the company Ralph worked for. Do you need to ask what kind of natural disaster happened to Ralph?

The second reason for playing straight with your customers is that—surprise!—customers respect honesty. No, it isn't fun to tell a customer that there is a problem, or that the delivery date the customer has in mind is unrealistic. But when you have to, yet make it clear you will follow through to do all in your power to make things right again, your customers come away appreciating you as a straight shooter they can depend on to tell the truth—regardless.

Miss Manners, a.k.a. Judith Martin, dubbed The High Priestess of Protocol by *Frequent Flyer* magazine, provides a case in point. She described two recent airline flights, both delayed due to bad weather. As she described them to the readers of *Frequent Flyer*:

> On the first, the crew did little to inform the passengers of the flight's status, glumly responding to requests for pillows, blankets, drinks, etc. The second crew apologized for the delay, offered advice on passengers' scheduling problems, kept everyone informed, and generally tried to make things as pleasant as possible.

Which planeload of passengers believed that the flight crew was really doing everything possible to get them to their destination? And which airline will Miss Manners choose the next time she flies?

Do It for Yourself Too

There is actually a third reason for always being honest with customers: the way you feel about yourself. A friend of ours used to work for a now defunct television shopping network company. She was the chief upset customer handler. When customers called in to report that the merchandise they bought was defective, her job was to smother those callers with "I'm sorry" and "we apologize" verbiage.

The trouble was, most of the merchandise the company was selling was factory seconds—items known by everyone in the company to be defective in some small way. Our friend was, in essence, a "shill" charged with the responsibility of mollifying the few customers who were brave enough to complain about their purchases. The company, she was told straight out, was counting on the fact that only about 4 percent of upset customers complain when they receive shoddy service or merchandise.

Did she give the complainers their money back? Absolutely. The company was willing to buy off the few who braved its complaint and return systems. Did she make the complainers feel better? Definitely. At least someone was there to listen to them.

But she quit her job after six months. Why? "Because," she says, "I couldn't take being part of an operation that was knowingly exploiting its customers."

TIP: How you feel about yourself in your job is as important to your personal self-esteem as the way you feel about yourself as a parent, a spouse, or a friend. No job is important enough to lie for, no paycheck big enough to compensate for feeling bad about your treatment of another human being. Perhaps the best reason to be honest with your customers is that it allows you to be honest with yourself.

Whoever is careless with the truth in small matters cannot be trusted with important matters.

—Albert Einstein

12

All Rules Were Meant to Be Broken

(Including This One)

Rules exist to serve, not enslave.

—Software programmer's axiom

Rules are everywhere. We encounter formal rules in the form of laws and policies: "No right turn on red," or "Returns must be accompanied by receipt." Other rules are informal, taught by custom or experience: "When you bump into another person, say 'Excuse me,'" or "Allow extra time when driving during rush hour."

Rules should share a single purpose: to make life run more smoothly, more efficiently, in a more organized and orderly fashion. We sometimes call this purpose the spirit of the law. But rules don't always fulfill their spirit. In fact, sometimes they work against what we're trying to accomplish. That's why it's important for Knock Your Socks Off Service professionals to understand the rules that direct their efforts.

Rules vs. Assumptions

We are so used to rules in our lives that sometimes, when we don't know the answer or aren't comfortable making a decision on our own, we're tempted to make up a rule to fill the gap. Or, in the stress of the moment, we may borrow a rule from another setting that seems to fit our current situation.

For example, imagine you're a new cashier. A customer comes in and asks to write a check for twenty dollars more than the amount of purchase. You don't know what your store policy is, and there's no one nearby to ask. What do you do?

- You might assume that cashing checks for over the amount is against the rules and say no.
- Or you may borrow a rule from your last job and allow the customer to write the check for five dollars or ten dollars more.

Either option is tempting because it puts you in control of the situation and keeps you from having to say, "Gee, I don't know if you can do that." But not knowing all the rules is natural! In fact, not knowing and finding out— for yourself and for the customer— is one of the best ways to learn on the job. Instead of assuming there must be a rule that will make you say no, find out how to say yes.

A friend of ours remembers a business trip to Kansas City. She was working particularly long days. Back in her hotel room one evening, hungry because she skipped lunch, she reviewed the room service menu. Nothing appealed to her. She called room service and asked if she could have a plain broiled chicken breast with a small salad. "I don't see that on the menu," the room service waiter responded. "It's not," she replied, "but it's what I'd really like to have. Can you make it?" Silence. Then again, "Well, it's not on the menu." To make a long story short, she didn't end up with a room service meal that night. But the room service personnel at many hotels since then have easily and cheerfully accommodated similar requests. Guess which hotel in Kansas City she tells people to avoid?

Red Rules vs. Blue Rules

Rules are important when they protect the public safety or reflect experience that says dire consequences will occur if the wrong things happen. But other rules are simply habits and customs with hardened arteries—systems that grow inflexible with age and take on a rigidity never intended.

In healthcare, some organizations we know of explain to employees that there are two kinds of rules—Red rules and Blue rules: *Red rules* are rules that cannot be broken. They are there to protect the life or well-being of the patient, for example, no smoking on the premises. *Blue rules* are designed to make the hospital experience run more smoothly for patient and staff alike, for example, incoming patients are processed through the admitting department.

Healthcare workers have to know when a Blue rule, such as "fill out the admission forms first," should or must be broken. For example, in the emergency room in certain situations, such as when a pregnant woman arrives in labor—then the paperwork can wait.

Do you know the Red rules and the Blue rules in your company? Red rules may be set by the government in the form

of laws or regulations or by your company's management. Blue rules may evolve from department policy or past experience. You need to understand where the rules come from and why they exist. Most important, you must be able to explain them to your customers so they in turn know why you're doing what you're doing.

> **TIP:** As you discuss Red rules and Blue rules in your own organization, there are bound to be disagreements about which is which. That's okay. A key outcome of your Red and Blue discussion is learning why a rule is a rule in the first place. For example, some employees at a large insurance company were upset to learn that using personal software programs such as screen savers and games on company computers was a violation of a Red Rule—actually a firing offense. After a very public e-mail dialog with the information services group about why the rule existed, most employees came to agree that there was indeed a danger of introducing a computer virus into the system. Now the color of that particular rule makes sense to everyone in the company.

Breaking vs. Bending the Rules

Know your own limits. If you believe an exception should be made, but aren't sure you can or should do it, ask a more experienced peer, your supervisor, or your manager.

Without formal and informal rules, service would become chaotic—and customers would never know what to expect. Just because you think that breaking or bending a rule won't cause the ceiling to fall doesn't mean you should take it lightly. Know the nature of the rule in question, the reason for the rule, the consequences of not following it, then help your customer make the system work.

> The exception proves the rule.
> —Seventeenth century proverb

13

Creating Trust in an Insecure, Suspicious World

For years and years we've told our customers they can trust us. It's up to each one of us every day to earn our customer's trust and respect.

—Don Cannon
Senior Vice President of Food
Merchandising, Wal-Mart Stores

Trust is the platinum standard of customer service. It is the glue that keeps customers coming back. The customer's faith in your word and belief in your promises are what saves you in those difficult times when everything seems to be going wrong. If you have made promises in the past and things have turned out well, the customer will trust you when things go from good to bad to worse.

Customer trust grows slowly, develops over a period of time, and is a succession of positive experiences. Trust can be dashed by a single incident of unfaithfulness and can be cemented by a singular memorable act.

Fairness is one of the customer's most critical trust-creating hot buttons. Treat me unfairly—from my point of view— and lose me forever as a client. What is fairness from the customer's point of view? That can and often does vary from customer to customer. But in general customers feel treated fairly when:

- They have the outcome they expected—they get what they asked for.
- The process of getting what they wanted was painless.
- You kept the performance promises you made—if you said you'd call by the end of the day, you did.
- You treated them ethically—no bait and switch, no sneaky behavior.
- You acknowledged their unique wishes if there were any.
- Their best interests were placed ahead of the company's convenience.

Example

It's 3 P.M. Friday afternoon. Mrs. Impulsive calls your travel agency. She just has to be in San Francisco by noon tomorrow. You warn her it could be expensive but you'll do your best. An hour later you have a coach class, excursion fare ticket on a 6 A.M. flight in hand. You call her with the news.

Question

The next time Mrs. Impulsive is up for a trip and needs someone she can depend on, who do you suppose she will call?

How Do You Build Trust?

Trust builds slowly, over time and through positive experiences. But there are some things you can do to speed trust along.

- *Practice frequent communications.* "Mrs. I, this is pretty short notice, I don't know if I can succeed, but I'll give it my best."
- *Develop openness.* "Good news! I had to ask for a little

favor and I had to go ahead and book you immediately, but if you can make a 6 A.M. flight, it is going to work out.

- *Show warmth.* "I hope you have a wonderful time. I know your daughter is going to be so glad and so surprised you could make it."
- *Stick with the truth.*"Given the few flights available on Saturdays, I might not be able to find one. But I'll do everything I can. The chances I'll succeed are pretty good."

There can be a fine line between fibbing to a customer and being reassuring. Telling the customer that "everything will be fine" when it might turn out otherwise is an unacceptable way of dealing with a situation. Being straightforward without overdramatizing risks or overemphasizing things that can go wrong is always a better course.

- *Show confidence.* If you seem hesitant to do what the customer wants done or unsure of yourself, you erode trust, even if you succeed. A simple, "I don't know if we can make that change this close to your flight, but let me take a look. Can I call you right back or would you rather I just put you on hold?" goes a long way to demonstrate your confidence.

Trust and Recovery

The core of the psychological side of recovery is restoring trust; the customer's belief that you can and will keep both the explicit and implicit promises you make. Dr. Kathleen Seiders says that trust is particularly at risk when customers feel *vulnerable*; that is, they perceive that all the power to set things right is in your hands and little or nothing is under their control. That sense of vulnerability—and the customer's reaction to a service breakdown—is the loudest when the customer feels he/she lacks the following:

Information. They don't know what is going on, or how long it will take to set things right.

Expertise. The customer couldn't fix the car or the computer or the fouled–up reservation on a bet. All the "smarts" are on your side of the table.

Freedom. There is no option for fixing the problem aside from dealing with you. The customer perceives you as the only hope.

Recourse. The customer perceives that when it comes to this computer or car or malady it's you or nobody. They may be free, contractually, to ask anyone else they can find to do the problem "fix," but there is no one else, or at least they see it that way.

Restoring trust is accomplished by involving the customer in solving the problem: "Tell me again exactly what was happening when the mower stopped," or "Can you give me a run-down on the history of this problem," reassuring the client that the problem is fixable and will be fixed.

When the customer feels vulnerable, trust is imperative.

—Leonard L. Berry
Service Expert

14

Do the Right Thing . . . Regardless

Use your good judgment in all situations.
There will be no additional rules.

—Nordstrom, Inc.
Employee Handbook

Doing things right and doing the right thing are separate but equal issues in providing Knock Your Socks Off Service.

Doing things right deals with the process of getting work done—doing your job correctly, using technical skills and people skills, learning about your company's products and services, and being able to answer questions about how things work and why, processing complaints or submitting orders or fixing things for the customer.

Doing the right thing is about deciding what the best thing to do is in a given situation. It involves making judgments about how to use your company's products and services on your customers' behalf—sometimes in ways they may not have asked for, or even thought of. It is about deciding whether or not to comply with a customer request.

The *Nordstrom Department Stores' Employee Handbook* is almost legendary. Its elegantly simple, solitary rule is: "Use your good judgment in all situations." The lack of additional rules doesn't mean there's no direction. Nordstrom employees—those fabled Knock Your Socks Off Service professionals—are encouraged to use their managers for support when they're not sure what to do. In Nordstrom's words:

> "Please feel free to ask your department manager,
> store manager or division general manager any ques-
> tion at any time."

In orientation and training programs, Nordstrom people
learn what doing the right thing means for the customers they
will serve. Sometimes it means accepting a return with no
questions asked or walking a customer to another department—even to a competitor's store—to find just the right
clothing accessory. The result? From coast to coast, people tell
stories about service, Nordstrom style. Even those who've
never seen the inside of a Nordstrom store have heard the stories thanks to books like *Fabled Service* written about Nordstrom. And just about the time they start to shake their heads
and say things like, "Sure, but how long can they stay in business doing things like that?" someone adds the real clincher:
Nordstrom regularly posts some of the highest sales per square
foot in the retail industry. Not only does nobody do it better,
nobody makes more money doing it right, either!

Is the Right Thing Ever Wrong?

Many front-line service workers and plenty of managers feel
an instinctive fear of simple policies such as, "do the right
thing." The fear is natural; for generations we've been warned
about the dire consequences of "giving the store away." But
that fear is easily overcome when common sense and the competence that comes with experience are brought to bear on the
subject.

> **TIP**: Take time—perhaps an hour every two weeks—
> to get together with your coworkers to learn from
> each other's experiences. Share stories of suc-
> cesses and failures with tough customer problems.
> The chances are very good that if you are having a
> problem with something, so are others.

Are you going to give the store away? Of course not, no more than Nordstrom's people do. When managers and service professionals feel uncertain about the idea of "do the right thing," we tell them the point of Knock Your Socks Off Service is to delight their customers. That makes customers come back again—and that makes money for the company.

It's pointless for your company to hire good people like you, train them well, back them with customer-friendly systems and supportive management, only to refuse them the opportunity (or see them decline the opportunity) to make good judgments on their customers' behalf. The system's not out of control; it is being controlled by *your* innate good sense. That's why your company has already entrusted you with its most priceless asset—customers, the very future of the business.

Your own good judgment applies in every industry. If you know your job, but aren't sure exactly what you should or shouldn't do in a particular situation, try using the following three questions as your guide:

1. Does the action violate a Red rule, or is it about bending a Blue rule? If a Red rule is involved, you can generally stop right here. When housekeepers at St. Luke's Hospital in Milwaukee are asked by patients for water, they know to check first with the charge nurse. If the patient is on restricted fluids, the simple act of providing a glass of water violates a Red rule.

2. If it involves a Blue rule, will bending or breaking the rule allow us to serve customers better? The fact that you *can* bend a rule is not in and of itself a compelling argument that you *should* bend or abandon a Blue rule. Interior window cleaning for the historic Foshay Tower in Minneapolis, Minnesota, has always been done during the work week, during normal business hours—a de facto Blue rule. While the building manager will happily schedule weekend service for tenants who need it, she first explains, "Our windows date from 1929. We prefer to clean during the week so that if we discover that a repair is needed, it can be done immediately. I don't want any tenant to suffer with a taped up or boarded up temporary fix."

3. Who should make the final decision? Find that person and take action. In many cases, it will be you. Sometimes, especially when bending a Blue rule involves a risk or an added expense, you will need to involve a manager or supervisor. With your answers to questions one and two, you will be able to offer your manager thoughtful perspective and an action plan.

> If they (employees) make a wrong decision, that's something that can be corrected later. At least they acted in good faith. This is part of our commitment (to our customers).
>
> —Isadore Sharp
> Chairman, Four Seasons Hotels

15

Listening Is a Skill—
Use It

Listening is about trust and respect and involvement
and information sharing more than it is about ears.
　　　　　　　　—Beverly Briggs
　　　　　　　　Editor, *Customer Connection Newsletter*

Most of us listen to only about 25 percent of what we hear.
What happens to the other 75 percent? We tune it out. In one
ear and out the other, as if we never heard it. Listening is so
important, it's amazing how seldom we practice it well. But
since good service involves listening, understanding, and responding to customers, good listening is an important skill for
practitioners of Knock Your Socks Off Service. When you listen well, you:

- Figure out what your customer wants and needs.
- Prevent misunderstandings and errors.
- Gather clues about ways to improve the service you pro-
  vide.
- Build long-term customer relationships.

It's important to listen actively, almost aggressively. To
serve your customers well, you need to know as exactly as
possible what they want, how they want it, when they want it,
what they expect to pay for it, how long they expect to wait,
and what else they expect with it. There's no need to guess—
and risk being wrong. Customers are ready, willing, and able

to tell you everything (or almost everything) you need to know.

Good Listeners Are Made, Not Born

People who seem to be natural listeners weren't born that way. They just started practicing a lot earlier. It's never too late to start improving because good listening is a skill that gets better as you exercise it. What's more, the listener has a powerful advantage in any conversation: While most people speak at only 125 to 150 words per minute, we can listen at up to 450 words per minute! That means we have time while listening to identify the main points the speaker is trying to make and begin to organize those points into an effective response.

> **TIP:** Reinforce listening to your customer by writing down information and ideas on how to respond—but don't dilute your focus by trying to formulate a rebuttal or argument. When you have a chance to speak, you will be able to "reflect" back your customer's key points. Reflection, even of the easy and obvious things, confirms that you have listened and understood your customer and are now ready to respond to the request, question, or problem.

Make sure you hear what the speaker is trying to communicate:

1. If the information is complex, confirm your understanding by repeating it: "Okay. Let me catch up with you. You've made some important points and I want to make sure I understand. You said that you..."

2. Ask questions if you are unclear about anything: "Do you want the multifaceted jumbo widget with the reverse locking knob or the superfaceted minimodel with the glow-in-the-dark handle?"

3. Read back critical information—for example, the spelling of the company's name or the numbers in a street address, phone number, web site, or e-mail address—after you write it down. It assures you are right and reassures the customer that you listened and heard.

Barriers to Effective Listening

A wide variety of distractions can get in the way of good listening.

- *Noise.* Too much noise in your business environment causes interference. Can you easily hear customers when they speak in a normal tone of voice? Or are they drowned out by too-loud music, the general hubbub of your workplace, or the voices of your coworkers and other customers?

- *Interruptions.* Communication happens when two people work at it together. Have you ever tried to explain something to someone who was constantly saying, "Just a sec, gotta take this call" or looking over your shoulder to yell advice or information to a colleague? Such controllable interruptions tell customers, "You aren't important," or "I really don't want to listen to you."

- *Daydreaming.* Interruptions come from inside as well as outside. When you find your thoughts drifting away to the movie you plan to see tonight or the fight you had with your sweetheart this morning, that internal interruption can be every bit as destructive to good listening as working in a foundry. Keep the focus on your customer.

- *Technology.* Technology can hinder effective listening as much as it can help to put us in touch. For all the good service made possible by telephones, voice-activated terminals, and remote microphones in drive-up windows, it's much harder to listen to someone you can't see face to face or whose voice is distorted by a machine. That monitor on your desk can get in the way as well. Rather than trying to listen to the customer and look for her account, you can simply say, "Okay, Mrs. Smith, let me get your account up on my screen...There it is. Now, let's go over that so I can capture all the details."

- *Stereotypes.* When we label people—when we make assumptions about what they look like, how they will behave, and what they have to say—we make it difficult to understand what they're really saying. From that false start, we fit what we later see, experience, and hear into a flawed prejudgment. And quite often we're very wrong.

- *Trigger words and phrases.* All of us have hot-buttons that customers may inadvertently push. And once the button is pushed, listening can stop. Remember that your main concern is to listen to what your customer is trying to say, not the individual words he or she uses. What rubs you the wrong way just may be completely innocent from the customer's perspective. (And even if the customer is giving you a dig over past performance, letting it pass shows your good grace and style.)

- *Attitude.* Your attitudes color what you hear and how you respond. Defensive people evaluate everything, looking for the hidden messages. People on the offensive are too often looking for a fight, formulating "oh-yes-well-let-me-tell-you" arguments even before the other person is finished speaking. Your attitudes should help you listen, not deafen you to a customer's words.

It's also important to listen for the things that you don't hear, the things your customers aren't saying to you. If customers used to compliment you on speedy delivery, but haven't recently, perhaps your performance is slipping. If they sigh and say, "Oh, fine, I guess," when you ask them how your services measure up, you should be hearing another message loud and clear.

> People don't buy because they are made to understand. They buy because they feel understood.
>
> —Sales Maxim

16

Ask Intelligent Questions

It is better to know some of the questions than to know all of the answers.

—James Thurber

Customers are often less than articulate—or even clear in their own minds—about their wants and needs. The customer who says "I'm not quite sure," in response to your "How may I help you?" is at least being frank and represents the feelings of a lot of customers. It's your job to help them sort it all out.

To be successful with the unsure or unclear or confused customer, you have to put on your detective hat. And like Sherlock Holmes, Jessica Fletcher, Miss Marple, Columbo, or the criminalists on CSI, you have to go in search of clues. Armed with a supply of good questions, you are sure to succeed.

Three types of questions will help you in your search for clues to what the unsure customer needs from you.

Background Questions

Background questions are the introduction to your conversation. They tell you who you are talking with and allow you to pull up a customer's profile or account. They also help you evaluate whether you are the best person to help the customer, or if you should direct him or her to a different person or department.

70

- "Do you have an account with us?"
- "May I have your customer identification number as it appears just above the label on the back of the catalog?"
- "I have a few questions about your past medical history. First, have you had any of the following ....?"

Sometimes, customers resist background questions. "Why do you need to know that?" they ask. Or they may protest, "I gave you that information the last time I was here. Don't you keep records?" You can decrease resistance by explaining up front why you need the information. We call this tactic *previewing*. Here are some examples:

- "I appreciate your concern Ms. Wilson. If you will just help me by answering a few questions, I'll get you connected to the best agent for your situation."
- "I need to ask you some questions about your medical history. We do this every visit to ensure that our records remain accurate and up to date."

The *preview* reassures your customer that you do care and that the background questions do have a purpose.

Probing Questions

Probing questions help you delve more deeply into a customer need, problem, or complaint to identify the issues involved and begin to move toward a solution. There are two basic types of questions: closed and open-ended. Closed questions are generally answered with a "Yes" or "No" or with a specific piece of information. A background question asking "What is your account number?" is a good example. Open-ended questions generally require more lengthy explanations and invite the customers into a conversation. More often than not, probing questions will be open-ended.

- "Can you tell me more about your event; who will be attending, what they will be expecting, and how last year's event could be improved upon?"

- "What features are you looking for in a new bike?
- "What happened after you plugged in the VCR?"

Remember that probing questions are a way for you to ask for information. If the answer your customer gives sounds impossible or untrue, don't dispute it. Instead, ask another probing question.

A good source of probing questions are the basic five Ws: who, what, when, where, and why. They've served reporters well for decades.

- "*Who* was affected by this?"
- "*What* would you like to see happen next?"
- "*When* do you need to have the new part installed?"
- "*Where* did the original part break?"
- "I'd like to find out *why* this happened so we can prevent it from happening again. Have you formed any theories?"

The exact questions you should ask will, of course, vary with the situation. And when in doubt, know you can almost always use the tried-and-true, all-purpose probing question, "Could you tell me more about that?" **NOTE:** Be careful using "why" questions, they can sound like you are accusing the customer of something or blaming them for the problem they are reporting.

Confirmation Questions

Confirmation questions provide a "check and balance" system. They help you confirm that you've correctly understood the customer's message, and they give the customer an opportunity to add additional information or clarification.

- "That takes us through the aftercare regime Dr. Kling prescribed. The exercises are the most important part and they can be challenging. Would you like to review them again?"

- "So, if we could provide you with a partial order today, enough product to see you through Monday, will that solve your immediate problem?"

It's easy to take silence as confirmation of customer agreement. However, silence sometimes signals that the customer has given up, is frustrated or angry, or is too embarrassed to indicate confusion. So, when your confirmation comes out as a statement, rather than as a question, it's a good idea to ask for a response, such as:

- "Let me make sure that I have the details right. You aren't actually moving in until the fifteenth, but you'll be doing work on your new home before that. Therefore, you need to have the new telephone working by the eleventh, and you don't want your old telephone disconnected until the sixteenth. Is that right?"

TIP: If you've ever had someone fix you in the eye and ask "Do you understand?" in a slow and deliberate voice, you know how demeaning some questions can sound. Monitor your words and tone so that your confirmation doesn't communicate, "Only an idiot wouldn't understand this. Are you an idiot?"

When Questions Go Wrong

The right question that is poorly timed or badly worded can undo all of the customer service magic you've worked so hard to create. When questions go wrong, typically one of four things has happened.

1. The question was asked at the wrong time; possibly out of sequence. There is a logic to the order in which questions should be asked. For example, it's generally easy to ask a customer's name early in the conversation and often very awkward to do so after the two of you finish a thirty-minute conversation.

2. The customer thought you were asking about something you already know; or that the customer believes you should know. Use the preview technique to explain why you need to ask.

- "I know that Hector has your number, but could I take it down again for quick reference?"

3. The customer feels you are asking too many questions. Make your questions count, for you and for your customer.

4. The question feels too personal. What's personal and what's just conversation will vary from person to person. If you're asking because you're curious, it may be better not to. If you're asking because you need the information, use the preview technique to explain why before you ask.

- "In order for us to build the best financial plan for you, I'll need to ask you some important questions about your personal finances. Of course, all the information we work with today will remain confidential. Do you have any questions before we begin?"

Only when you begin to ask the right questions do you begin to find the right answers.

—Dorothy Leeds
Smart Questions: A New Strategy for Successful Managers

17

Winning Words and Soothing Phrases

Politeness goes far, yet costs nothing.

—Samuel Smiles
Nineteenth-century popular writer

"Oh yeah?! Sticks and stones may break my bones, but words will never hurt me." Sound familiar? As children, we recited those words many times. They were our self-defense in the very situations where we learned that words did hurt—emotionally, if not physically. And many of us carry memories that remind us that the pain words inflict can be more devastating than any bruise or broken arm.

Words are just as powerful to adults. We are capable of bruising or soothing our customers with words; it all depends on how we use them. The service professional who can use words well gains a distinct advantage in the service transaction.

Forbidden Phrases

Some words, alone or in combination, create immediate negative images. Nancy Friedman, a customer service and telephone skills consultant known to many by her business persona, "The Telephone Doctor,™" advocates a ban on what she calls Five Forbidden Phrases—five responses that, intentionally or unintentionally, can drive your customers right up the wall in anger or frustration. They are listed in Table 17-1, with her suggested alternatives.

Table 17-1.

Forbidden Phrase	Use Instead
1. "I don't know."	"Gee, that's a good question. Let me check and find out."
2. "We can't do that."	"Boy that's a tough one. Let's see what we can do." Then find an alternative solution.
3. "You'll have to..."	Soften the request with phrases like, "You'll need to," or "Here's how we can help you with that," or "The next time that happens, here's what you can do."
4. "Hang on a second; I'll be right back."	"It may take me two or three minutes (or however long it will really take) to get that. Are you able to hold/wait while I check?"
5. "No" when used at the beginning of any sentence.	If you think before you speak, you can turn every negative answer into a positive response, "We aren't able to refund your money, but we can replace the product at no charge."

While those five phrases are sure to raise customer ire, they aren't the only ones. What phrases not listed in Table 17-1 would rile you as a customer?

TIP: Create your own list of Do Say and Don't Say words and phrases. Use the list from Table 17-2 to get started. From your own experience and the insight of your coworkers, you can add many more of your own. What words and phrases are guaranteed to bring a smile to your customer's face?

Which ones create a frown? Add to it from your own experiences as a customer and as a service professional. (Note: All of the examples come from real-life situations (Table 17-2).)

Table 17-2.

Don't Say	Do Say
"She went to get another candy bar."	"She's not available right now."
"Are we through yet?"	"Will there be anything else?"
"No problem"	"It will be my pleasure," or "I'd be happy to."
""Honey" or "Buddy" or "Lady."	The customer's name (the way he or she wishes it to be used).
"Well, that's not really my concern."	"I understand how upset you are."
"Yeah, yeah, I'll get to it."	"I'll take care of that for you personally."

The Message Behind the Words

Every Knock Your Socks Off Service professional has times when something said in all sincerity or innocence to a customer, something that sounds reasonable and rational to you, causes the customer to explode with anger. It's not the intent of your words to create customer anger, but it is the effect. As you learn to notice some of the common words and phrases that provoke these undesirable responses, you'll find yourself becoming more successful at avoiding or defusing such situations.

One of the most common negative messages we can send to customers is, "I think you're stupid." We send that message when we use phrases like, "Do you understand?" with that certain tone of voice, or when we begin talking to a customer as if we were addressing a four year old (even though the customer's behavior may be straight out of preschool). If four year olds don't appreciate being talked down to, why should adult customers find it enjoyable or satisfying?

A cable TV technician described a helpful technique to ensure understanding without demeaning the customer in the *Customer Connection Newsletter*. The technicians needed to make sure the customer on the phone was starting from the right point:

> Before I can help (a subscriber) with a problem, it's important for me to confirm that the set is tuned in to the right channel. . . . When I ask "Is the TV tuned to channel 3?" the customer answers "Yes" automatically . . . and I'm uncomfortable saying "Please go and check." So now I say, "Will you please go to the TV set and turn it to channel 5. Wait for ten seconds then turn it back to channel 3. Then come back and tell me what happened." This gets the action I need without having to challenge the customer's word.

This method also doesn't communicate that the technician thinks the customer really doesn't know how to operate a TV.

Scripting the Panic Away

Telemarketers, those people who call you at dinner to sell you things, for years have used scripts: prewritten conversations intended to help the telemarketers put their best foot forward.

Service people are often reluctant to use scripts for fear that they will sound robotic or mechanical in their interactions with customers. And that can happen. But it doesn't have to.

Service consultant Gail Boylan, former chief nurse at Baptist Health Group in Pensacola, Florida, used to feel the same way: "I hated the idea of scripting. It seemed like an insult to people's intelligence." Nonetheless, encouraged by what she saw in an award-winning hospital in Chicago, she and her colleagues wrote some simple scripts—phrases everyone could use with patients—that had a dramatic effect on customer perceptions of service and caring.

One group of nurses came up with the idea of saying, "I'm closing this curtain to help protect your privacy." When curtaining off a patient's bed. Patients began remarking on how caring and concerned the staff was.

Before leaving a patient's room, room cleaning people, nurses aids, and maintenance people began saying, "Is there anything else I can do for you. I have the time right now to help you." Comments about how considerate the staff was were suddenly heard all over the hospital. As important, the number of nonmedical calls from patients to the nursing stations decreased by 40 percent.

Service scripts work best when:

- They are short and easy to remember.
- They are developed around issues that are important to customers.
- They can be paraphrased—people are permitted to put them into their own words.

The best service scripts? That's easy. Those are the ones you and your colleagues sit down and write for yourselves.

Man does not live by words alone, despite the fact that sometimes he has to eat them.

—Adlai Stevenson
Lawyer and politician

18

Facts for Face to Face

I solemnly promise and declare that for every customer
that comes within ten feet of me, I will smile, look them
in the eye and greet them, so help me Sam.
—Employee Pledge, Wal-Mart Discount Stores

The words we speak, hear, or read are only a small part of the way we communicate with one another. Experts suggest that in face-to-face situations, at least 70 percent of what is communicated is done without speaking a word. This is called nonverbal communication.

What is nonverbal communication? It's everything we don't say—our body language, what we do, how we act and re-act, and what we show to others when we are with them. There are nine basic dimensions of nonverbal communication. Knock Your Socks Off Service professionals are keenly aware of each.

1. *Proximity.* Carry on a conversation with a coworker while standing about an arm's length apart. After a few minutes, move forward until your noses are about six inches apart. Feel uncomfortable? Most North Americans will. The same will be true if you're standing six feet apart. "Comfort zones" vary from culture to culture. Most North Americans prefer to maintain a distance of between a foot and a half and two feet as their "space." Europeans, except for the English, tend to be comfortable standing closer. The same goes for most South Americans.

2. *Eye contact.* Making eye contact acknowledges that you see, and are dealing with, your customers as individuals, that you are paying attention. There's a balance to be struck here: People who don't make eye contact in our culture are considered shifty or even dishonest, but staring can make your customers uncomfortable, too. And eye contact in Europe, Asia, the Middle East, Mexico and South America is governed by specific cultural rules.

3. *Silence.* You can and do communicate even when you're saying nothing. Remaining silent while your customers are talking is a basic courtesy, nodding tells them you're listening and understanding what you hear. Prolonged silence, however, can leave customers concerned that either you did not hear them or that you disagree with what they said. An occasional "uh huh" or "I see" tells them you're still listening without interrupting.

4. *Gestures.* Closed gestures such as tightly crossed arms, hands tucked deep in pockets, or clenched fists create non-verbal barriers. Open gestures invite people into our space and say we're comfortable having them near us. Many of our gestures are unconscious (some people cross their arms when they're cold, for example), so make a point of thinking about what you're doing nonverbally when you deal with customers.

5. *Posture.* "Stand up straight," your mother always said, and she was right. Good physical posture conveys confidence and competence. Leaning in slightly when customers are talking says you think what they are saying is important and interesting.

6. *Facial expression.* We all know the cues: a raised eyebrow communicates surprise; a wink indicates sly agreement or alliance; tightly set lips, opposition; a wide open smile, friendliness. Your face communicates, even when your voice doesn't.

7. *Physical contact.* What is and is not appropriate today varies greatly with the situation and the people involved. A handshake is customary, but placing a hand on another person's arm or an arm over someone's shoulder can be a very

personal act. The rule of thumb is "less is best" in most professional situations.

8. *Smell.* This is perhaps the least understood of our senses, but an important one in service work that involves getting close to customers. Be just as careful with strong perfumes and colognes—some customers may be sensitive or allergic—as you are of the natural odors they are used to cover up. Be aware, too, that at a time when fewer than one in three adults smokes, the lingering smell of tobacco can be offensive.

9. *Overall appearance.* Just as in a theatrical performance, you have to look your part. Whether your costume is a three-piece suit or blue coveralls depends on the job you do, what you want to communicate to customers, and especially what your customers expect to see. Whatever the case, one thing will always be true of your physical appearance: Cleanliness and neatness communicate competence. (Messy people may be just as, if not more, competent than neat people, it's true, but they will have to work a lot harder to prove it to the customer!)

Nonverbal Cues

TIP: Sometimes the nonverbal messages we send are more powerful, more persuasive, and more revealing than the words we speak. When our nonverbal signals send a different message than our words, our customers can become confused; disoriented; or skeptical of our motives, actions, and interest in serving their needs. A significant part of your success as a service professional will come from how you manage your face-to-face, nonverbal communications.

The flip side of nonverbal communication is knowing how to read the nonverbal cues of your customers. Almost everyone can look at other people and read their obvious body

language. We know when others are happy or sad, calm or upset.

What makes one person appear so at ease in social situations or in dealing with customers, while others seem uncomfortable, unaware, or inept? Research suggests that the difference may lie in what we do with what we know. Socially adept individuals more readily accept and act on the body language signals they see. Others plow blindly ahead, unmindful of the confused looks that say, "Please stop and explain that again."

Customers may not always speak up when they feel uncomfortable or confused or frustrated. But if you "listen" for the messages, you pick up the nonverbal cues as well as the audible ones. Use them effectively and they'll help you meet and exceed your customer's needs and expectations.

Perception is the key to nonverbal success.

—Sales training axiom

19

Tips for Telephone Talk

If I pick up a ringing phone, I accept the responsibility to ensure the caller is satisfied, *no matter,* what the issue.

—Michael Ramundo
President, MCR Marketing, Inc.

Using the telephone requires you to be more aware of your voice than at any other time. Customers cannot hear your facial expressions or see your nonverbal clues—like shrugs or hand gestures. They do form a mental picture of you based on the tone and quality of your voice. Your mood—smiling and happy or tight-lipped and angry—often comes through. That's why, before you ever pick up a telephone, you should take a moment to be sure that you are mentally prepared to deal with the customer on the other end. A pleasant phone voice takes practice. This Telephone Style Checklist (Table 19-1) can help you assess your phone style. After all, speaking in well-modulated, pleasant tones is a learned talent.

> **TIP:** Tape-record yourself talking on the phone, then ask an honest friend or your boss to evaluate your vocal quality. Better yet, have someone tape you from the listener's end so you can listen to how you sound to your customers.
> **WARNING:** If you have never heard yourself on audiotape before, you will be surprised at the way you sound. Don't let it bother you: We all sound strange to ourselves on tape.

Table 19-1
TELEPHONE STYLE CHECKLIST

Vocal Quality

	Yes	No
Voice is easy to hear without being too loud.	☐	☐
Words are clearly articulated.	☐	☐
Pacing is good—neither too slow nor too fast.	☐	☐
Vocal tone is pleasant—neither grating nor nasal.	☐	☐
Energy level shows interest and enthusiasm.	☐	☐

Phone Techniques

	Yes	No
Phone is answered quickly—on the second or third ring.	☐	☐
Caller is greeted courteously.	☐	☐
Representative identifies self to caller.	☐	☐
Transfers are handled professionally.	☐	☐
Messages taken are complete and accurate	☐	☐

Telephone Etiquette: A Quick Review

Professional telephone talk has four basic customer sensitive processes. Knowing and following them will ensure that your customers feel you are really taking care of them.

Answering the Phone

The ringing of a telephone is one of the most insistent sounds in the world. (Just try to let your home phone ring without answering it. Most people can't.) When a customer calls and no one answers, or the line is busy, or it rings fifteen times before someone picks it up, it's like telling the customer (as one phone company television ad says), "I'm sorry, but you will have to take your money and leave the store. We are very busy here and we just don't have time to help you. Please go shop somewhere else. And thank-you for trying to do business with us." Set a standard for yourself (two or three rings, for example) and try to meet it every time.

When you pick up the phone, remember that your customer can hear you from the moment the handset leaves the cradle. You wouldn't want your customer to be greeted with, (*distant voice*) "So, I told her a thing or two... (*direct voice*) Oh, hello."

> **WINNING PHRASE:** "Hello, you've reached Acme Inc. This is Monica. How may I help you?" The best greetings contain three elements. First, a greeting, like "Hello" or "Good morning." Because some phone systems cut off the first word, the greeting protects the second element, the identification statement. *Crime Stopper's Hint:* Practice saying your identification statement slowly. Too often the identification is so rushed, the caller doesn't know who he or she has reached, "HelloAcmeAcresHowMayIHelpYou" is not one word— it just sounds like it when delivered by a bored service rep.

Entering Information

Frequently customer calls require that you look up information or enter information into a computer system. When you are doing that face to face the customer sees you working away and almost automatically exercises patience and paces the information flow accordingly.

Over the phone, the customer can't see your fingers flying across the keyboard. To give yourself the time you need to bring up the customer's account, find the information the customer needs or to enter the customer's data, subtly cue the customer by describing what you are doing. Phrases like:

> "Okay, Mrs. Smith, let me get your account up on my screen. . . Here we are. Okay. I see here you placed that order on the fifteenth. . . ."

And

> "Let me get that entered into my computer here. Okay, that's 35185 Virginia Drive, Sychamore, s-y-c-h-a-m-o-r-e, Indiana, "

Working aloud—talking as you are entering customer information or bringing up her account—lets the customer know what you are doing and assures her that you haven't put her on hold and walked off to get coffee.

> **CAUTION:** Don't make a part of your small talk comments about the speed, or lack of it, of your system. That suggests your company is out of date and raises doubts about your reliability. Tell the caller who he or she has reached. Finally, ask how you may be of assistance.

Putting a Caller on Hold

Sometimes callers have to be put on hold. You may need to answer a second line, you may need to leave your desk to get information, or you may just need a moment to regroup while handling a particularly volatile caller.

Whatever the circumstances, never put a caller on hold without first asking permission: "May I put you on hold?" or "Will you hold, please?" And the question means nothing if you don't wait for the answer. Yes, it takes a moment longer. But it is well worth it for the positive impression it creates. And yes, you risk hearing, "No, you may not." Accept that and either reprioritize things or take the caller's number and call back as quickly as possible.

The caller who doesn't want to hold is not necessarily being pushy. Recently, a good friend of ours phoned her doctor's office. Because the receptionist knew her, she assumed she could just park her on hold with an "Oh, Nancy, hang on a minute," while she handled another call. That assumption was almost fatal. Nancy had just crawled to the phone after suffering a major medical problem.

Her case is a rare one, to be sure, but callers may have other legitimate reasons for not wanting, or not being able, to hold. Remember that Knock Your Socks Off Service is delivered individually to match what each customer needs and expects.

> **WINNING PHRASE:** When you are juggling multiple calls and need to put nonemergency calls on hold, use "Are you able to hold?" instead of "May I put you on hold?" Customers will often respond yes to the "Are you able" question, even when holding is not what they prefer to do.

Taking Messages

Good messages are accurate and complete. Be sure to get the caller's full name, company name, and phone number. "Tell her Bill called" only works if the person the message is intended for knows only one Bill. To make sure you have the correct spelling of the caller's name and an accurate phone number, read it back. The date and time of the message is also important. Finally, be sure to put your own name on the message; if there is any question, the message recipient will be able to ask you for clarification.

> **WINNING PHRASE:** "May I have your phone number for quick reference?" Customers sometimes resent leaving their phone numbers—"He has it. After all, I'm returning his call." The "for quick reference" phrase will help you bypass that negative response and take a complete message.

Transferring Calls

Customers hate to be passed from pillar to post to Pammy to Paul and back again. Whenever possible, don't do it: Help the caller yourself or take a message and have the appropriate person return the call. When you do have to transfer a call, be sure to give the name and phone number of the person who will help them. This way, if there is any problem with the switch, the caller will be able to get back to the right person. And if you can, stay on the line to be sure the transfer goes smoothly.

> **WINNING PHRASE:** "Jose, I'm transferring a call from Mr. Polasky to you. He needs an update on his account." Let the person you are transferring the call to know who is on the line and why you're transferring the call. One caution: Always talk about the caller in respectful terms—never assume your customer can't hear you simply because he or she is supposed to be on hold during the transfer.

Voice Mail

Voice mail is both the biggest boon and the biggest bane of modern business. We have a real love/hate relationship with this tool. To use voice mail in the best possible way, remember the following guidelines.

- Voice mail is not a substitute for, but a supplement to, real-time phone communication. When you have the option, always try to talk directly to a customer, rather than leave a message or a series of messages.
- Change your message frequently, providing up-to-date information about whether or not you are in, when you will pick up and return messages, and who the caller might contact if the request can't wait.
- Tell callers what information to leave. Some systems automatically "tag" incoming messages with the date and time. If your system doesn't, you may need to remind callers to provide that information.
- Let your callers know how to use your system. "To indicate that your message is urgent, press 1." Or, "In the future, you may skip this message by pressing the pound key.
- Listen to your message periodically to ensure that the message is clear and that the voice mail system is working properly. They can break down, fill up, and malfunction.
- Return messages promptly. Many customer service reps follow the sundown rule: Return all calls within the same day.

Taking full advantage of the benefits of telephone talk requires that you understand and can easily use the features on your telephone system, and that you craft your phone communication as carefully as you craft your face-to-face encounters.

Teleconferencing

Whether you are a participant in a teleconference—more than two people connected to a single phone conversation—or are simply making the connection for the meeting, there are some important protocols to remember.

1. Once the time and date for the teleconference is set, make sure everyone who will be participating has the dial-in instructions and meeting time. "Double-click" that information: phone and e-mail it to the participants.

HINT: If the teleconference is scheduled for more than 7 days in the future, then be sure to e-mail participants a reminder the afternoon before the teleconference—if it is an A.M. teleconference—or the morning of the teleconference if it is a noon or afternoon call. And if the teleconference crosses time zones which they usually do, specify the start time by time zone. For instance: If the teleconference is being set up by a person in Chicago, and all the participants will be from the United Sates, your notes to participants should specify central time zone: "The conference call will begin at 10:00 A.M. CST."

2. Introductions are important for making the most of conference call time and to avoid confusion. If you are the conference call originator, be the first one to connect and have a printed list of participants in front of you. As you hear people joining the call, ask them to identify themselves: "I believe someone just joined us. This is Sara from ABC Widget. Could you identify yourself?" And as others join, let them know who is already on the line. For instance: "Thank you for joining us. Bill Gras and Mary Hadder are also with us. Bill is vice president of the color widget division and Mary is director of customer service. Bill and Mary, could you say hello?"

HINT: Think of a teleconference as a meeting in a large windowless room during a power outage. Your job is to help everyone find a seat and get comfortable with the other participants.

3. Once everyone is in—online— take a few seconds to establish the ground rules. Here are two:

- If there are more than four people in the meeting, people should be asked to identify themselves when they speak, as in: "This is Sara. I couldn't agree with you more, Bill. And I'd like to add. . . ".
- If there is an agenda ask participants to have it in front of them.

4. Review assignments and follow-up activities before everyone signs off—hangs up—and the conference ends. Follow-up with an e-mail confirming everyone's commitments and assignments.

5. If this is a client conference, do not review the meeting with your colleagues on the conference line. Hang up and call everyone back, or, if you all work in the same facility, meet face-to-face. Never postmortem a tele-meeting on the conference line. You cannot be sure everyone has hung up. Avoid the potential embarrassment of saying something you wouldn't want the client to hear while they are still on the line!

When you answer the phone, your store's image is on the line.

Headline
Video Business magazine

20

Putting Pen to Paper

The writer who does the most gives his reader the most knowledge, and takes from him the least time.

—Charles Caleb Colton
Nineteenth-century English cleric

Verbal communication is quick and personal. It allows you to convey information and confirm immediate understanding while you observe the customer's body language and probe for additional questions or concerns. But verbal communication is not always possible.

Sometimes, written communication is required, or is just a good idea. You may not be able to reach the customer by phone or in person. You may need to send additional information. You may want to create a paper trail that can help both you and your customer track a service transaction that has spread out over several weeks or months. Even if there's no immediate need, a letter after a conversation with a customer can be a terrific way to confirm facts and details—not to mention to say thanks.

As with other aspects of Knock Your Socks Off Service, there are elements of style and substance that should be combined on your customer's behalf whenever you put pen to paper. While some of the written material your company sends to customers (from bills and advertising flyers to product documentation and legal notices) is necessarily standardized and impersonal, a more personal tone should come through in your own written communications.

Your Message

Why are you writing to your customer? Because you have something to say and a reason to say it:

• *You write to confirm understanding.* Suppose, for example, you're a travel agent. A couple wants your help in planning a winter vacation. They explain that they want to go to Colorado to ski, but don't want to stay at a big resort. They'd like to try to rent a condo—and it would be great if you could get one that was "no smoking." Having a spa and pool close by, as well as shopping, is important. And, of course, they want to get the cheapest possible package price.

It's a tall order. To fill it, you'll spend time discussing which of their requests are must-haves, and which are simply boy-it'd-be-great-if-we-coulds. And to show you're really on the ball, you follow up with a letter that outlines your discussion. The letter confirms the details for you both and makes your customers feel like you really listened.

• *You write to create documentation.* A paper trail can confirm what action was or will be taken after the verbal conversation is over. It can serve as a quick summary of activity several months from now when your memory of the transaction has started to get a little fuzzy around the edges. It can even act as a contract, binding you and your customer to a particular agreement as to how to handle a given situation.

• *You write to solidify relationships.* Written communications are a way to make tangible (and memorable) the fleeting, transient nature of most service interactions. A thank-you note gives tangible evidence of your care and appreciation. An FYI or useful clipping from a current newspaper or magazine makes it clear you're thinking about your customers, even though you haven't seen them personally in a while. An "attaboy!" letter when something good happens to your customers (or their companies) says there's more than just money involved in the relationship.(See Table 20-1.)

Table 20-1
EIGHT LETTER-WRITING TIPS

1. Whatever the content or purpose of your letter, make it neat and legible.
2. If you are writing on the record for your company, type or word process your letter on company letterhead.
3. Unless you are sending a quick personal note, use standard $8^1/_2$ by 11 inch paper. Smaller pages are more easily misplaced in filing; larger ones don't fit into the basic spaces of the modern office: in-baskets, file folders, copiers and faxes, and briefcases.
4. Get to the point quickly. State your purpose for writing in the first paragraph.
5. Be brief. Try to keep letters to one page whenever possible.
6. Write in the first person. *I* rather than *we*.
7. Write the way you speak. Your letter should sound as if it comes from a real person, not a bureaucrat.
8. Write right. Spell words correctly. Use proper style and grammar. If you're not sure, ask someone else to proofread for you and suggest ways to polish your prose.

NOTE: If you are writing in cyberspace—sending electronic mail—be sure to consider the e-mail tips that follow in the next chapter

Words fly, writings remain.

—Latin Proverb

21

Putting Your Best E-Mail Foot Forward

When you introduce yourself via e-mail, not only are you making a first impression, you're also leaving a written record.

—Virginia Shea
Netiquette™ Guru

Today many organizations regularly communicate with their customers via e-mail. Sometimes that e-mail comes through the company's commercial web site, other times it comes through an Internet Service Provider (ISP) like America Online, Hotmail, or Earthlink.

Regardless of the route the e-mail follows to get to your screen, there are both customer expectations and e-mail protocols to observe when you are providing customer service by e-mail over the World Wide Web. Customers judge online service by how easy a company is to contact and how quickly and accurately questions are answered. And while your company may have a fabulously robust Frequently Asked Question (FAQ) section on its web site, customer opinion of the site's customer service will more likely be based on the quality of your response to their e-mail questions and complaints. The e-mail response is a transaction between customer and company that the customer can, and does, use to judge the company's concern for his or her needs and problems and the company's responsiveness skills. In short, in the customer's eyes, you are the company even in the age of the Internet.

The Internet/E-Mail Customer

Just as the over-the-phone customer doesn't think much of you if their call isn't answered in one or two rings, the e-mail customer isn't impressed if it takes two or three days to receive a reply. Think of it this way: If someone put you on hold for two days how happy would that make you? Customers expect e-mail to be almost as fast as the telephone. After all, they reason, the whole thing works by computer, shouldn't it be fast?

> **TIP:** The standard reply time expectation for business e-mails is about 8 hours, but headed down. If you can't make a same day reply to a customer inquiry you should at least acknowledge receipt of the message the same day. Some web sites do this automatically. If yours doesn't, acknowledge the message and tell the sender when you will have a reply.

Replying to E-Mails

Many people are used to "conversing" in a chatty, informal way with their friends over the Internet. Be careful! Do not treat customers like old friends—unless they are. And take care in the language you use with customers. Unless you are writing to someone who is very familiar with your business, avoid jargon and shorthand expressions—your customer may not know what a POS display or XD29 system is. It's also dangerous to assume that anyone who sends you electronic mail is familiar with all of the uniquenesses and conventions of e-mail. For example, people who use e-mail frequently often use acronyms, such as IMHO (In My Humble Opinion) and BTW (By the Way), and put "emoticons," symbols that convey emotions, in their correspondence. Here are few of the most popular emoticons:

    :-) = Smile; "I'm joking"
    :-(= Frown, "I'm sad"
    :-() = Yelling; Shocked
    <g> = Grin

WARNING! Avoid these conventions unless you have seen them in the customer's correspondence with you. Even then, it is safest to avoid them if you have any doubts.

Think about the characteristics of the person you are sending the e-mail to:

• Is your reader a child or an adult? Young or old? Is English his or her first language? Make sure your customers will understand what you write and be comfortable with the way you write it. Even with young, Internet savvy customers, loose language and flip remarks can be misunderstood.

• What's the nature of your relationship with this customer? If you haven't corresponded with this customer much, be more formal. If the customer is upset with something don't try "kidding" or cajoling them regardless of how well you know them.

Reread your correspondence before you push "send." Look at the tone. A cold, impersonal tone, for instance, tells

customers you're thinking of them like a number. Too much jargon and legalese will confuse rather than comfort and make them wonder if you have something to hide. And spelling counts in e-mail as well. If you didn't care enough to spell check, what does that tell the customer?(See Table 21-1.)

The Outcome

Think about the action you want to encourage. It should be clear from what you've written why you are writing and what,

---

Table 21-1
THREE E-MAIL TIPS*

1. Be personal. While e-mail to customers should be more formal than e-mail to friends or coworkers, e-mail users have come to expect electronic communication to have a more personal style. One way to add interest is to use "emoticons," sometimes called "smileys," in the text. "They're easy to figure out once you get the hang of it," writes e-mail advisor Virginia Shea. "Just remember that they're all sideways faces."
2. Think like a 1950s Smith Corona typewriter. (If you don't know what a typewriter is, ask your supervisor to explain.) Shea notes that you shouldn't expect e-mail systems—yours or your customer's—to accurately communicate the common "special effects" of today's written documents. That means no boldface, italics, underlines, or tabs. Stick to the standard ASCII characters—the twenty-six upper and lower case letters of the alphabet, the numerals 0 through 9, and most commonly used punctuation marks. Shea also suggests limiting e-mail line length to sixty to eighty characters or eight to ten words to avoid annoying line breaks.
3. Don't YELL. Using all capital letters to communicate is the e-mail equivalent of constant bellowing. While caps may be used for emphasis, consider other methods, such as surrounding text with *asterisks* to indicate italics, or __underscores__ to indicate underlining.

*Adapted from Virginia Shea, *Netiquette*, (Albion Books, 1994).

---

if anything, you expect your customers to do in response. Do they need to take any action? If so, by what date and in what form? Are they supposed to retain the correspondence for future reference? If so, for how long? Do they need to pass it along to someone else? If so, to whom and by when? Good writing is an extremely powerful part of good service. Inept writing undermines everything you've worked so hard to build.

Personalization

When you are responding to e-mail queries, personalized messages hold much more value than computer-generated responses in the customers' eyes. The personal response tells the customer that you are interested in helping them do business with you. If your company has an Internet shopping site, personalization is the most obvious, straightforward way to uplift the shopper's experience. A study by the Forrester Research firm found that 37 percent of all online shoppers—4.8 million shoppers—expect customer service online, primarily through e-mail. And they base their opinion of the company on the way their inquiries and problems are responded to. Consider the following customer e-mails and the customer service representative responses—these are "real-life" examples—and think of where they could serve as models for making your customer correspondence more personal.

From a customer:

> Hello,
> I'm considering ordering a holiday Fab Five Cookie Wreath—even though it's after Christmas. Will it last until next Christmas or will it decay? I couldn't tell if it was a real or permanent wreath.

The reply:

> Dear Disney Guest,
> Thank you for your e-mail. Below is the information you requested regarding item A20228, the Fab Five Cookie Wreath.

Because the wreath has sugar cookies on it, the cookies will probably not be good by next Christmas. The actual wreath is a faux wreath and is not real, so you can enjoy that for many years to come.
If we can be of any further assistance, please let us know.
Sincerely,

DisneyStore.com

From a customer:
Hello,
I'm considering purchasing a seven-wood golf club—can you tell me how this will improve my game?

Dave

The reply:
Dave,
A seven-wood takes the place of your three iron. You can also use it out of the rough if the ball is sitting high, but normally it will take the place of the three iron. On long tough shots where the ball will be hard to get up in the air, it will take its place. It is good off the tee and long Iron shots, and it could win you some money, too! Hit'em long and straight!
    Have a great day!
    Andrew Reichert
    Fogdog.com

The Ultimate Sports Store

She's thrilled to be answering 95% of customers' e-mails within 3 days. (Doesn't she know that within hours most went straight to her competitor's sites?)

—Genesys Advertisement

22

Exceptional Service Is in the Details

It is just the little touches after the average man would quit that make the master's fame.

—Orison Swett Marden
Founder, *Success* magazine

Asked about the difference between memorable and mundane buildings, Swiss architect Mies van der Rohe responded simply, "God is in the details, the details, the details." What's true of quality architecture is true of quality service: If you pay attention to the details, the right details, customers will know, and notice, and come back for more.

Everything Counts

The details surround us, no matter what kind of job we do. It's how we look, and how our workplace looks. It's how we speak and what we say. It's all the little extra courtesies and comforts we build into the service experience—or the myriad nagging annoyances we lose track of and make our customers wade through to do business with us.

Attention to details is a prime characteristic of high-performing organizations. The cast members at Walt Disney World have a passion for details that make customers sit up and take notice. A friend of ours raves about Shirley, the housekeeper she met during a recent vacation to Walt Disney

World. "The first day, when we checked in, I saw the `Your room was cleaned by Shirley. Have a great stay' note. I noticed the `I' in Shirley was dotted with a little Mickey. That was cute, but we were at Disney. The third day Shirley really wowed me. I'd left a note asking for more towels. When we returned to the room, there was a "Do not disturb" sign on our bathroom door. Inside, Shirley had taken our morning paper and the eyeglasses I'd left by the sink, and arranged the extra towels in the form of a man sitting on the toilet reading the daily paper. "I laughed so loud. I don't think I'll ever forget that!"

A growing number of managers and executives today understand the examples they set in turn sets a positive tone for their organizations. For example:

- Fred Smith, the founder and chairman of FedEx, begins many of his visits to FedEx facilities in far-flung cities by hopping on a delivery van and going out on the road with a FedEx courier.
- Bill Marriott, Jr., chairman and CEO of Marriott International, often takes a turn at the hotel registration desk checking in guests; he also empties ashtrays in the lobby and picks up trash in the parking lot.
- And there isn't a manager at Walt Disney World or Disneyland who doesn't personally pick up, straighten, and worry after the thousand and one details that create an unparalleled experience for their customers.

These executives model attention to detail for their employees, just as you model it for customers and coworkers.

The Moments of Truth

Attention to detail is more than playing at or being a janitor. It is the way you remember—and remind others—that contact with any aspect of your work group gives your customers an opportunity to form or revise their impressions, positive or negative. We refer to these opportunities as Moments of Truth:

A Moment of Truth occurs anytime a customer comes in contact with any part of your organization and uses that contact to judge the quality of the organization.

Anything and everything can become a Moment of Truth for your customers: the look of your store, building, or parking lot; the promises made in your advertising; how long your phone rings before being answered, and how the call is handled; written correspondence and bills . . . plus the memorable personal contacts your customers have with you.

Managing the Moments of Truth

When you began your current job, your orientation and training probably focused on the primary moments of truth built into your position. If you have been with your company for a long time, you've probably learned to recognize many more Moments of Truth that are important to your customers. To deliver true Knock Your Socks Off Service, you have to manage each and every Moment of Truth individually.

> **TIP:** The way that Moments of Truth are managed determines the grades customers give you on their mental report cards. Manage the moments well, and you receive A's and B's—and earn a repeat customer. Manage them poorly, and you earn D's and F's—and lose a customer in the bargain. Work to get good grades in this particular school and you'll find your diploma has cash value.

Over time, it's easy to think you've mastered all the various moments of truth your customers might present you with. Don't you believe it! No matter how experienced and skillful you become, you can always count on your customers to come up with something new. That's because customers can turn almost anything into a moment of truth.

To truly master the Moments of Truth in your services, develop these three customer-focused habits:

1. *Never stop learning.* The details that are important to your customers change from day to day as well as

from customer to customer. There's always more to know.

2. *Ask your customers.* The only reliable way to identify your customers' particular, peculiar moments of truth is to get your customers to describe them to you.

3. *Ask your company.* In addition to your own informal, day-to-day observations of customer preferences, your company probably conducts continuing surveys and studies. Make sure you know what the researchers know that will help you serve your customers better.

It's not the tigers and bears that chase the customers away. What bugs the customer the most are the mosquitoes and the gnats—the little things.

Commit yourself to performing one ten-minute act of exceptional customer service per day and to inducing your colleagues to do the same. In a 100-person outfit, taking into account normal vacations, holidays, etc., that would mean 24,000 new courteous acts per year. Such is the stuff of revolutions.

—Tom Peters

23

Good Selling Is Good Service—Good Service Is Good Selling

Nothing happens until someone sells something.

—Marketing axiom

Sales and service are not separate functions. They are two sides of the same coin. Even if your title is customer service representative and a coworker is a sales associate, you both have the same ultimate goal: satisfying the customer. It wasn't always this way. In days gone by, sales and service personnel used to be adversaries.

Sales and marketing people viewed their counterparts in service and operations as "those guys who never want to help me make a sale and who screw it up after it's a done deal."

Service and operations folk, for their part, tended to view sales and marketing people as "those people in suits who write outlandish ads, make ridiculous promises to close a sale, and leave us holding the bag with the customer."

In today's world, sales, marketing, service, and operations share a common goal: creating and retaining customers.

When Lines Overlap

To create and retain customers we have to combine good selling with good service. Consider the case of Edgar Pinchpenny III, the unhappy owner of a Model 412-A Handy-Andy Cordless Electric Screwdriver. (You know he's unhappy because he is waving the 412-A around, banging it on the desk and demanding his money back.)

Using your very best Knock Your Socks Off Service skills (listening—questioning—problem solving), you determine that Pinchpenny is upset because the 412-A needs frequent recharging and isn't very powerful. But you also know that the 412-A was built for small repair jobs around the house. It absolutely was not designed for the industrial strength, barn-building, automobile overhaul sort of work Pinchpenny is trying to get out of it. That's why your company also sells the much more expensive 412-C Turbo-Andy, the best professional power screwdriver in the industry and the perfect tool for Pinchpenny's job.

Better service at the time of the original sale *might* have matched Pinchpenny with the more appropriate tool. But what should you do about the situation now? Tighten the chin strap on your thinking cap and consider which of these four possible actions you would recommend:

- *Option 1.* Tell Pinchpenny that if he hadn't been too cheap to buy the proper tools in the first place, he wouldn't be standing here screaming himself into a coronary.
- *Option 2.* Explain the limitations of the 412-A and the benefits of the 412-C to Pinchpenny, and recommend that he consider buying *up.*
- *Option 3.* Apologize to Pinchpenny for the inconvenience, explain the difference between the two models, and offer to personally make an exchange on the spot and give him a discount on the 412-C to compensate for being inconvenienced.
- *Option 4.* Apologize for the salesperson's stupidity, offer Pinchpenny an even exchange—the old, abused 412-A for a shiny new 412-C at no additional cost—throw in a free set of your best stainless steel screwdriver bits *and* offer to wash Pinchpenny's car.

We pick Option 3 as the best course of action: It shows concern, responsiveness, and good salesmanship. It doesn't unduly
punish Pinchpenny for the human error involved in the original purchase—whether his or ours. Nor does it unduly reward
him for his argumentative, and unpleasant, return behavior.
Option 2 is a narrow, old-fashioned, service-as-complaint-de-
partment response. It isn't likely to keep Pinchpenny as a long-
term customer. Options 1 and 4 are the kind of answers suitable
for companies where frontline people are specifically recruited
with IQs approximately equal to their shoe sizes.

When Selling Is Not Good Service

There are three situations in which selling is not good service.

1. *When there are no alternatives.* The customer's needs
   cannot be met by any product or service you offer, regardless of how well you can fix the problem, answer
   the question, or explain the current product or service.
2. *When there is no slack.* You know how to solve the
   problem, but the customer came to you mad, has
   stayed mad, and obviously wants to stay mad. There is
   very little chance to make the customer unmad, let
   alone sell an upgrade or a switch to a different model.
3. *When there is no point.* An upgrade or add-on would
   be totally illogical, unrelated, or inappropriate to the
   situation, as in, "Would you like some garlic bread to
   go with your cappuccino this morning?"

When Selling Is Good Service

There are five situations in which selling is good service.

1. *When the product or service the customer is using is
   wrong—but you know which model, system, or ap-*

proach will better fit the customer's needs and are in a position to get it for the customer.

2. *When the product or service the customer acquired from your company is right—but some other part, piece, program, or process is needed before your product or service will perform properly:* "Your computer operating system is Windows 95. Our software is designed for the new XP operating system. I do know of an upgrade for Windows 95 that might work."

3. *When the product or service in question is out of date.*"I can send you a new widget and walk you through the repair when you receive it. I also think it would be a good idea to consider a newer model that will do the job better. The Laser XJ7 has improved circuitry and can . . .."

4. *When an add-on feature will forestall other problems.*"I see you decided against extended warranty protection. Since you've had two problems during the warranty period, I wonder if you shouldn't reconsider that decision?"

5. *When changing the customer to a different product or service will be seen as value-added or TLC.* "This checking account requires a very high minimum balance. That's what caused the service charge you are concerned about. I'd like to recommend a different plan that I think will fit your needs better and save you from incurring future charges."

If it says customer service on your name tag, then serving the customer is your full-time occupation. But remember: Even if nothing in your job description hints at a sales responsibility, you are a part of the sales and marketing team. Yours is always a two-hat job.

In reality, selling and service are inseparable.

—Leonard Berry, David Bennett, Carter Brown
Service Quality

24

Never Underestimate the Value of a Sincere Thank-You

Thank-You . . . Thank-You, Thank-You . . . and Thank-You!!!

—Fozzie Bear

Remember when you were ten years old and what you wanted for your birthday was that electric train or special Barbie? And your grandmother gave you underwear instead. And your mom and dad stood there and looked at you and pinched you on the arm. "Now, what do you say?" they prompted. "Thank-you, Grandma," you said. And your grandma beamed and patted you on the head.

Saying thank-you is as important today as when your parents tried so hard to drum it into your head. In your job, you need to say thanks to your customers every day. You need to sincerely value the gift of business they bring you—even if it may not be as exciting as electric trains and Barbie dolls.

Nine Times When You Should Thank Customers

1. *When they do business with you . . . every time.* It bears repeating: Customers have options every time they need a service or product. It's easy to take regular and

walk-in customers for granted. Don't. Thank them for choosing to do business with you.

2. *When they compliment you (or your company).* Compliments can be embarrassing. But shrugging off customers' sincere praise says, "You dummy, I'm not really that good." Instead, accept it gracefully, say, "Thank-you," and add, "I really appreciate your business."

3. *When they offer comments or suggestions.* Thanking customers for feedback says that you've heard what they had to say and value their opinion. Something as simple as "Thank-you for taking the time to tell me that! It really helps us know where we can do better," delivered with eye contact and a smile, can work wonders.

4. *When they try a new product or service.* Trying something new can be uncomfortable—and risky. After all, the old and familiar is so, well, old and familiar. Thank customers for daring to try something different.

5. *When they recommend you to a friend.* When customers recommend you, they put themselves on the line If you deliver, they look good. If you don't. . . . a written thank-you for a recommendation or a value-added token the next time you see those customers face to face says you value their recommendation.

6. *When they are patient . . . and not so patient.* Whether they tell you about it or not (and, boy, will some customers tell you about it!), no one likes to wait. Thanking customers for their patience says you noticed and value their time. It's also one of the quickest ways to defuse customers who have waited too long and are none too happy about it.

7. *When they help you to serve them better.* Some customers are always prepared. They have their account numbers right at their fingertips, always bring the right forms, and kept notes on their last service call. They make your life a lot easier; thank them for it.

8. *When they complain to you.* Thank them for complaining? Absolutely! Customers who tell you they are

unhappy are giving you a second chance. And that's quite a gift. Now you have a chance to win their renewed loyalty, which will give you additional opportunities to thank them in the future.

9. *When they make you smile.* A smile is one of the greatest gifts you can receive. Saying thank-you just makes it better.

Three Ways to Say Thank-You

1. *Verbally.* Say it after every encounter. And say it with feeling. The phrase "thank-you-for-shopping-at-our-store, next?" said like a freight train roaring past, doesn't impress customers. Make your thank-yous warm, pleasant, and personal.

2. *In writing.* Send a follow-up note after a purchase or visit. Personalize it. Customers hate form letters. Write a thank-you at the bottom of invoices or bills. Even thank- yous via e-mail correspondence are appreciated—though not as much as handwritten gratitude.

3. *With a gift.* Give something small, like a notepad or pen imprinted with your company name. It will help customers remember your business. For the right customer, an enjoyable e-mail graphic is a good thank-you card but be very careful and selective; tastes differ widely. (And beware, the computer fire walls in some companies might delete your greeting before they get to the intended recipient.)

TIP: Make sure the value of the gift isn't out of balance with the nature of the business involved. Some customers worry that more expensive gifts may be an attempt to buy their business, rather than a token of appreciation. Additionally, it's generally considered inappropriate to send a tangible

gift to a government client under any circumstance.

Five Often-Forgotten Thank-Yous

1. *Thank your coworkers.* Give credit to those who help you. Thank coworkers who, by the way they show concern for customers, serve as a role model for you. Doing this in front of customers at every opportunity tells customers they're dealing with a team effort.
2. *Thank your boss.* To make sure your managers give you the support you need, give positive feedback when they help you do your job.
3. *Thank people in other departments of your company.* While you may be the one actually talking to the customers, support people make the service you deliver possible. Thank them individually or as a group.
4. *Thank your vendors.* Without their professionalism, your customers wouldn't be receiving the satisfying service you're able to provide.
5. *Thank yourself!* You do a tough job and deserve a pat on the back. Give yourself credit for a job well done. And take yourself out for an extra special reward once in a while.

TIP: The most effective thank-yous are immediate, specific, sincere, and special.

Gratitude is not only the greatest virtue but the mother of all the rest.

—Cicero

III

The Problem-Solving Side of Knock Your Socks Off Service

ALL I Said was Yes.

SERVICE

Things don't always work out right. It's simply the law of averages. No matter how hard you try for perfection, sometimes you make a mistake. Sometimes your customer is wrong. And sometimes you just find yourself dealing with a difficult individual—someone who is never satisfied and tests your patience as well as your skills.

When things go wrong, it's time to play your trump card— your Knock Your Socks Off Service problem-solving skills. Being able to solve problems—to rescue the situation when it appears bleakest—is a key element in providing great service. It makes your job easier. It makes your company's business run smoother. And it's also a tremendous way to mend relationships with your customers and make them even more loyal.

25

Be a Fantastic Fixer

Customers don't expect you to be perfect. They do expect you to fix things when they go wrong.

—Donald Porter
British Airways

You go into a department store to buy a camcorder only to find that the advertised model is sold out. You are disappointed— even angry. *Why did they advertise it if they didn't have it?!* you ask yourself. A salesperson notices your obvious upset. Maybe it's the expression on your face—or the steam coming out of your ears.

Salesperson: May I help you?

You (grumpily): I doubt it. I wanted an EZ-Use Camcorder, but you people never have the stuff you advertise!

Salesperson: I'm sorry. We sold more than we expected before the ad ran, so we only had a couple left this morning. But we *are* offering a rain check, and we'll have the EZ-Use back in stock in about four weeks.

You: Oh, great. Four weeks will be two weeks after my daughter's wedding. That's just dandy.

Salesperson: I can see that you are disappointed. It's frustrating to want something and then to learn that we don't have it in stock. If you'll wait here for two minutes while I check with my manager, I think I can help you today. (*Two minutes later:*) Great news. I can offer you another manufacturer's comparable model for the same sale price. That way you can take your camcorder home today.

Beaming, and maybe slightly surprised, you leave the store with a new camcorder, two backup batteries, a special lighting package, an extended warranty, a half dozen videotapes, and a new bag to carry it all.

The Art of Service Recovery

The word *recovery* means to return to normal—to get things back in balance or good health. That's what the store's sales associate just did for the upset would-be camcorder buyer. In service, good recovery begins when you recognize (and the sooner the better) that a customer has a problem.

> **TIP:** Problems exist when the customer says they do—anytime the customer is upset, dismayed, angered, or disappointed. And what constitutes a disappointment for one customer can be absolutely "no problem" for another. No matter. You can't wish (or order) a problem away because it is something no reasonable person would be upset about, or because it's not your fault, or it's not your company's fault, or even because the customer made a mistake. If the customer *thinks* it's a problem—it's a problem.

Being a Fantastic Fixer, a real Knock Your Socks Off Service problem-solving professional, involves taking thoughtful, positive actions that will lead disappointed customers back to a state of satisfaction with your organization. Healing injured customer feelings requires sensitivity to their needs, wants, and expectations.

The Recovery Process

Once a customer problem is identified, the service recovery process should begin. Not all of the six steps described here

are needed for all customers. Use what you know about your company's products and services, and what you can discover about your customers' problems, to customize your actions to the specific situation. One size doesn't fit all.

1. *Apologize.* It doesn't matter who's at fault. Customers want someone to acknowledge that a problem occurred and show concern for their disappointment. Saying, "I'm sorry you have been inconvenienced this way" doesn't cost a dime, but it buys a barrel of forgiveness.
2. *Listen and empathize.* Treat your customers in a way that shows you care about them as well as their problem. People have feelings and emotions. They want the personal side of the transaction acknowledged.
3. *Fix the problem quickly and fairly.* A "fair fix" is one that's delivered with a sense of professional concern. At the bottom line, customers want what they expected to receive in the first place, and the sooner the better.
4. *Offer atonement.* It's not uncommon for dissatisfied customers to feel injured or put out by a service breakdown. Often they will look to you to provide some value-added gesture that says, in a manner appropriate to the problem, "I want to make it up to you."

NOTE: Atonement is not a requirement for successful recovery from every service or product breakdown. Rather, atonement is critical to satisfaction when the customer feels "injured" by the service delivery breakdown, when the customer feels victimized, greatly inconvenienced, or somehow damaged by the problem.

5. *Keep your promises.* Service recovery is needed because a customer believes a service promise has been broken. A product hasn't arrived. A callback hasn't occurred as promised. During the recovery process, you will often need to make new promises. When you do, be realistic about what you can and can't deliver.

TIP: Take immediate steps to solve problems. The sense of urgency you bring to problem solving tells your customers that recovery is every bit as important to you (and your organization) as the initial sale.

6. *Follow up.* You can add a pleasant extra to the recovery sequence by following up a few hours, days, or weeks later to make sure things really were resolved to your customer's satisfaction. Don't assume you've fixed the person or the problem. Check to be sure.

Asking for Trouble

Do we really need to even talk about when things go wrong? Why not just put our energy into doing it right the first time? Because it won't always go right the first time. In fact, about a third of all the problems service providers have to deal with are caused by their customers. Service, even Knock Your Socks Off Service, involves human beings, and human beings are never 100 percent perfect. That's true for your customers, and it's true for you. Mistakes happen. We all know it. Even when you do your job correctly and satisfy the customer's need, a problem can occur if expectations are not met.

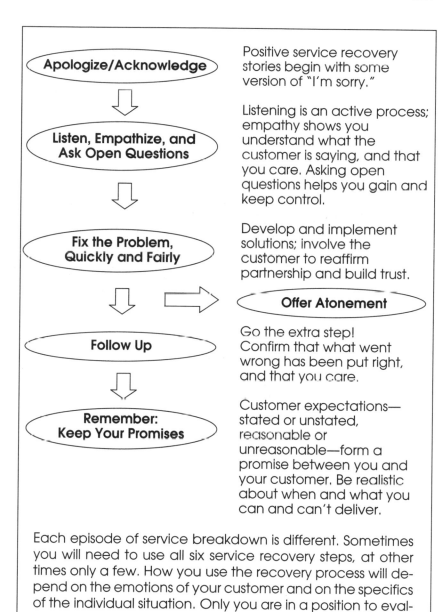

Apologize/Acknowledge

Positive service recovery stories begin with some version of "I'm sorry."

Listen, Empathize, and Ask Open Questions

Listening is an active process; empathy shows you understand what the customer is saying, and that you care. Asking open questions helps you gain and keep control.

Fix the Problem, Quickly and Fairly

Develop and implement solutions; involve the customer to reaffirm partnership and build trust.

Offer Atonement

Follow Up

Go the extra step! Confirm that what went wrong has been put right, and that you care.

Remember: Keep Your Promises

Customer expectations—stated or unstated, reasonable or unreasonable—form a promise between you and your customer. Be realistic about when and what you can and can't deliver.

Each episode of service breakdown is different. Sometimes you will need to use all six service recovery steps, at other times only a few. How you use the recovery process will depend on the emotions of your customer and on the specifics of the individual situation. Only you are in a position to evaluate and act.

Figure 25-1. The Service Recovery Process

No matter what happens, or why, it is better to handle the occasional mishaps directly and effectively than to ignore them in hopes they'll go away, or to muddle through while hoping for the best.*

Three Rules of Service Recovery

1. Do it right the first time.
2. Fix it if it fails.
3. Remember: There are no third chances.

—Dr. Leonard Berry
Researcher, Texas A&M University

*For more on service recovery read, Ron Zemke and Chip R. Bell *Knock Your Socks Off Service Recovery* (AMACOM).

26

Use the Well-Placed "I'm Sorry"

A few words of regret is a way of saying you care, a show of sensitivity to the ragged edges of another's emotion.

—Robert Conklin
How to Get People to Do Things

The words are so simple—"I'm sorry"—yet we hear them far too infrequently. In fact, our research shows that when customers tell a company about a problem with a product or service, they receive an apology less than half the time. That's about half as often as they should. The solution to every problem, whether major or minor, should start with a sincere apology.

Why is it so hard for us to say "I'm sorry" to our customers? First and foremost, we may be intimidated by the words. We may think that "I'm sorry" actually means "I've failed," "I'm not a good person," or "I'm not professional." Nothing could be further from the truth. An apology is simply an acknowledgment that things aren't going right in your customer's eyes.

Legal Jeopardy

Today, there is also a tendency to equate being sorry with an admission of personal or corporate liability—that being sorry means you are somehow to blame. Megabuck lawsuits are

123

common stories from the six o'clock news to prime-time entertainment programs. It's understandable that companies worry about the potential financial consequences of an apology and individuals are reluctant to take the blame personally.

If your job has legal or regulatory aspects, make sure you understand what they are and how they affect what you do. But don't assume that you're not allowed to say, "I'm sorry you were inconvenienced," when a snafu occurs. Actually, a sincere apology, delivered in a timely and professional manner, often goes a long way toward heading off potential legal problems. When you show your willingness to make sure your customers receive what they expect to receive, you relieve them of the need to even think about starting a fight.

Customer Jeopardy

Just as apologizing is not an admission of responsibility ("I'm sorry *we* did this to you"), neither is it an opportunity to place blame ("I'm sorry *you* were too stupid to read the directions before turning it on and shorting it out").

We all know that customers don't always use their own common sense or the painstakingly detailed directions we give them. Sometimes, for whatever the reason, they do it wrong—with predictably disastrous consequences. They look to us to fix it. And since no one likes to admit a mistake, they'll often blame us in the process.

When Vision Cable of Charlotte, North Carolina, was hit hard by a hurricane a few years ago, thousands of customers lost cable service. Vision Cable employees did everything they could to restore service as quickly as possible. Crews worked day and night. But general manager Milton Moore also personally apologized to customers in a series of radio ads, assuring them they would receive credit for every day they were without service and asking for their help in reporting any additional service interruptions.

Did he have to do that? Of course not. But his customers heard the message loud and clear: Let's all get things back to normal as quickly as we can. If Moore can apologize for a hurricane, just think how much you can accomplish with a well-placed, "I'm sorry."

> **TIP:** A sincere apology is a personal and professional acknowledgment that your customer was disappointed or inconvenienced. When saying the words "I'm sorry" feels like taking on too much of the blame, consider saying "Thank you for bringing that to my attention," instead.

Scapegoating

When things go wrong, there's an almost instinctive urge to direct the customer's attention elsewhere: "If those 'smart guys' in computer services could ever figure out how to make this system work the way it's supposed to, we wouldn't have to put you through long waits like this," or "Maintenance was supposed to clean that up last night, but I guess they were too busy taking a coffee break. So you ended up stepping in it."

TIP: Scapegoating another part of your organization for a service breakdown simply tells your customers that you're separate departments working in isolated and even adversarial ways, instead of a tight-knit team working for them. Don't do it—not to each other, not to yourself.

Do It Right

A vague apology delivered in an impersonal, machinelike manner can be worse than no apology at all. Effective apologies are:

1. *Sincere.* While you may not know exactly what your customers are feeling and experiencing individually, the way the employees of Vision Cable did, you can be genuine in your concern.
2. *Personal.* Apologies are far more powerful when they are delivered in the first person: "*I* am sorry that you are experiencing a problem." Remember, to the customer, you—not some mysterious "we" or "they," are the company.
3. *Timely.* Don't wait to find out why there is a problem or what caused it before expressing regret that the problem exists in the first place. The sooner you react to a distressed customer, the better.

I believe that if you are honest and straightforward with customers, they will treat you like a neighbor when circumstances beyond your control put you in a "one-down" position.

—Milton Moore
General Manager, Vision Cable

27

The Axioms of Service Recovery

Customers with problems have to go through a healing process before they can move on. The goal is to get the customer to say, "I'm really not happy about what happened, but I can't thank you enough for the support you provided to get me through it."

—Leo Colborne
Vice President, Global Tech Support
EMC Corporation

Customers have recovery expectations, just as they have expectations of normal service. Some of those are easy to guess at: fix the problem, be quick about it, and show a little empathy for my inconvenience. Other customer expectations are less obvious and more subtle.

The six-step process described in Chapter 25 rests on five axioms—five basic ideas about recovery—that come from what experts tell us customers expect of service recovery and our own research on the topic.

Axiom 1: Customers Have Specific Recovery Expectations

Research done in the retail banking industry by Linda Cooper of Cooper and Associates, Evanston, Illinois, found ten expectations of recovery. These ten expectations, listed in figure

27-1, could just as easily apply to service recovery situations
in other industries as well.

Top Ten Service Expectations of Bank Retail Customers
1. Being called back when promised.
2. Recieving an explanation of how a problem happened.
3. Knowing who to contact with a problem.
4. Being contacted promptly when a problem is resolved.
5. Being allowed to talk to someone in authority.
6. Being told how long it will take to resolve a problem.
7. Being given useful alternatives if a problem can't be solved.
8. Being treated like a person, not an account number.
9. Being told about ways to prevent a future problem.
10. Being given progress reports if a problem can't be solved immediately

Figure 27-1.

Axiom 2: Successful Recovery is Psychological as Well as Physical: Fix the Person, then the Problem

As we have said, customers who have a problem with your
product or service, expect you to solve the problem. Just as important, but less easy for customers to articulate, is the need to
be "fixed" psychologically. Often a customer who has a bad
experience with your company or product loses faith in you
reliability—you're ability to deliver what you promised. The
repair person who goes straight to the copier or laser printer,
completes the repair task, and quietly leaves for the next call
may be practicing good technical service, but not good recovery. The customer contact person who needed to use the broken machine and reported the problem needs to be "repaired"
as well. If nothing more, the service person needs to give the
customer an opportunity to vent his or her pent-up frustration.
It's part of the job.

Process wise, it is critical to fix—deal with and reassure
the customer that everything will be fine, *before* plunging into

the job of fixing the problem. The most important "customer fixing" skill you can develop is listening. Letting the customer tell their tale, blow off steam, and give you their point of view. Adding a sincere apology to the formula goes a long way toward creating a psychological fix.

Axiom 3: Work in a Spirit of Partnership

Our research suggests strongly that customers who participate in the problem-solving effort are more satisfied with the problem resolution. There are, however, limits and provisos to this idea. When your company has clearly caused the problem, asking the customer what he or she would like to see happen next gives the customer a sense of regaining control. That regained sense of control can be vital to calming customers who feel that the organization treated them unjustly or in some way abused them, or are bordering on a perception that they have been victimized or treated unfairly.

When the customer clearly caused the problem, asking him or her to do something to help solve the problem is appropriate and increases the probability that the customer will feel satisfied with the solution. The solution, in both situations, becomes "our" solution—one we create together and both own, not "your" solution—something you made up and are trying to sell me.

Critical to creating a sense of partnership is the way you invite the customer into the problem-solving process. The query, "So, what do you want me to do about it?" delivered the wrong way, can be seen as shifting your responsibility for service recovery back onto the customer.

Remember those old movies when the doctors send the father off to "boil water" in preparation for a home birth? By and large, the water-boiling assignment was a way of keeping the father out of the way, occupied, and feeling a part of the process. Even if all the customer can really do, metaphorically, is boil water, the effort has palliative effects.

The bank customer who failed to endorse her paycheck when she deposited it, and thereby caused a string of bounced checks, feels better about the recovery effort when given a part in fixing the problem. An assignment like "Give me a list of all

the people you've written checks to" or "call the people you've written checks to and ask them to resubmit them for payment" gives the customer back some sense of psychological control.

Axiom 4: Customers React More Strongly to "Fairness" Failures Than to "Honest Mistakes."

Researcher Kathleen Seiders, Babson College, Wellesley, Massachusetts,[1] has found that "When customers believe they have been treated unfairly, their reactions tend to be immediate, emotional, and enduring." In other words, if the customer feels he/she has been short changed, given short shrift, or been disrespected on purpose, the reaction is heated and long lasting.

[3] Kathleen Seiders and Leonard Berry, "Service Fairness: What It Is and Why It Matters," *Academy* of Management Executive12(1998):8-20.

There is but one course of action for you to take when the customer feels unfairly treated—extreme apology and atonement. Sure, the customer's feelings may indeed be the result of a misunderstanding of something said. That is irrelevant. Once a customer feels unfairly treated, you are dealing with an at-risk customer. According to Dr. Seiders, that is also a customer who is a prime candidate for hostile retaliation. Dr. Seiders adds that communication (explaining what went wrong) and compensation (atonement) can repair a perception of unfairness. It is important, she adds, to cast the explanation in terms that do not attempt to put the full responsibility for the faux pas on the shoulders of a third party or a "misunderstanding." The direct, simple, "I'm sorry this has occurred and I'll make sure it is cleared up right away" is as close to a magic bullet as there is in service recovery.

Axiom 5: Effective Recovery Is a Planned Process

Airlines and hotels overbook. Trains and planes have weather delays and cancellations so they plan ahead for these problems. If uncontrollable conditions can cause problems for your customers, creating a plan makes good sense. However, you must institute and apply the plan in a highly responsive, customer-sensitive fashion. Customers remember uncaring, robotic recovery long after they forget the incident that necessitated the solution.

It is important to know what a planned recovery process should be. You need to know what the organization's planned recovery process looks like—if there is one. If you are creating your own planned recovery, be sure to get input and agreement from others on your team, including your boss. It is also critically important that they regularly practice implementing the plan. Customers remember two things from well-designed and well-implemented planned recovery: the quality of the solutions offered and the skill of the people offering it. Of the two, the skill of the people delivering the solution—is the most memorable. What skills are those? We recently conducted eighty-one focus groups and asked participants to tell

What Focus Group Members Remembered and Found Impressive	Percent of Interviewees Who Commented on and Were Impressed by This Action
CSR dealt with my upset.	79.0
CSR apologized.	69.1
CSR didn't become defensive, but showed humility and poise.	62.9
CSR followed up after the complaint transaction.	56.8
CSR showed skill at problem solving.	53.0
CSR, when appropriate, was proactive in admitting organization error, didn't try to shift blame.	44.4
CSR acted in a fully responsible and empowered fashion on the customer's behalf	40.7
CSR showed good interpersonal skills, particularly listening.	40.7
CSR showed empathy for the customer's plight and/or upset.	38.3
CSR believed the customer, valued the customer's perception.	24.7

Figure 27-2.

us what they remembered and found impressive about recent recovery experiences. The top ten, most memorable service representative actions they experienced are listed in figure 27-2.

> You can't guarantee you'll never make mistakes.
> You can guarantee you'll fix them.
>
> —Jeff Bezos
> Founder and CEO, Amazon.com

28

Service Recovery on the Internet

*Why should I wait longer for an Internet web site
than I do a McDonald's drive through order?*

—Anonymous

No discussion of service recovery is complete without mentioning the new game in town: the Internet. Many customers have taken to the World Wide Web to sell their wares and serve their customers. Figures show that growing numbers of us now prefer to shop with a mouse rather than at a mall. Cambridge, Massachusetts-based Forrester Research predicts that Internet spending will jump to $7 trillion worldwide by 2004.

But plenty of those e-tailers, as well as "click-and-brick" companies–organizations with both stores and Internet sales sites—are still focused only on acquiring customers, not servicing them. Having a great web site is one thing, creating the customer support, online problem help, and other shopper-friendly features needed to keep e-shoppers coming back beyond one visit is quite another. That raises the stakes higher for good service recovery online and that's where you come in. Experts agree that the standard for customer service and problem solving is higher for the web than it is in the offline, face-to-face, and over-the-phone customer service. Why? Because customers think of the Internet and the computers that drive it as fast and easy and expect the service they receive over the Internet to be fast and easy.

Online shoppers start out with high expectations of the online shopping experience. Customers who can shop around the clock on the Internet now expect around-the-clock service, something they'd never think of demanding from a store. When they visit web sites and send out e-mail requests for help or more information, many expect a response within an hour or two—not realizing or caring that the service rep on the receiving end—you—might have received requests from a hundred other customers at the same time they received your request.

Companies in the e-commerce business need to stand ready to deal with a new strain of customer complaint: the "cybervent," or the complaint lodged via e-mail. Unhappy Internet customers find the detached distance of e-mail a license to complain more regularly—and often with more emotional fervor and in a nastier tone. According to a report in *USA Today* the National Consumers League received up to 1,000 online complaints a month in 1999, compared to just 600 per month in 1998. The Federal Trade Commission received an average of 4,800 online complaints a month in 1999, up from only 2,000 a month in 1998.

Preliminary Rules of the Road

While the rules for Internet service are still developing, there are some emerging guidelines. Here are a few simple ideas your organization should be looking at. Consider these things to look for in your company's Internet practice.

- *Easy customer access to phone numbers.* Far too many consumer Web sites don't list a phone number, or the number is difficult to locate. There should be an 800 number on your company's home page that is easy for e-customers to find – and someone at that number to help them. Take a look. If you don't see one or it isn't easy to find, bring that to someone's attention. If customers tell you the phone number was hard to find, report that as well.

- *One-click help.*Help for customers—whether it involves product availability, billing, order confirmation, delivery tracking, or other information—should never be more than one click away. Customers should not be forced to click endlessly into a carpal tunnel seizure to find what they need. If the customer can easily find these things on your web site, they are less likely to call you for that information. Go explore your company's web site. If it takes more than four clicks to find customer service and send a message, report that. If customers tell you they hate all the clicking they have to do—report that as well.

- *A list of frequently asked questions (FAQs).*FAQs take the pressure off live phone or online (e-mail) support by giving customers easy and around-the-clock access to the most commonly asked questions about your company. Some experts advise creating two layers of FAQs—one for prospective or new customers with fundamental questions, and another for continuing customers who are familiar with your products or services. Look your company's FAQs over. If the questions you are most frequently asked are not in the FAQs, report that. If customers tell you the answers in the FAQs aren't clear, report that as well.

- *Standards for e-mail response.*There should be clear, set standards for response time to e-mail inquiries and

clear guidelines for answering questions and addressing problems in customer-sensitive ways.

The web is an immediate medium, and long delays in response times can dull customer loyalty. Once a customer has
been disappointed by how slowly questions are answered or
problems resolved, they're not likely to try again.

Lands' End receives about 400 e-mail requests
daily, and staffers have a standard of responding
within three hours. At Dell Computer, support technicians answer most customer e-mails within four
hours. How do your company's standards measure up?

In the spirit of keeping online customers apprised and up-
dated on your work on their behalf, there should be some form
of "auto acknowledgment," a computer program that responds
to customers' incoming e-mail requests stating that the question was received and then sends back a response that is an es-
timate of how long it might take to answer the question. If your
company doesn't have one, ask why it doesn't.

- *Product return channels are synchronized and comple-
  ment each other.* Customers are none too pleased when
  they order product from a web site, only to find they
  can't return it at the company's store. Are your company's Internet return policies synchronized for easy
  in-person product return? If they aren't, you need to
  know why and what the two different systems are. Customers will ask.

Desert your online customers and they'll return the
favor.

—www.liveperson.com

29

Fix the Person

Here's your food and I hope you choke on it!!
—Fast-food server to a customer who complained
about waiting ten minutes to be served.
(It's true. We're not making it up.)

The toughest part of dealing with people, as you already know, is dealing with people. When products develop problems, customers have an object to curse, kick, yell at, and focus their feelings on. When a service breaks down, however, the focus of their emotional reaction is on you.

It is tempting to respond in kind to the emotional fireworks set off by disgruntled customers. Tempting, but not very wise, and certainly not very productive. Meeting anger with anger, sarcasm with sarcasm, frustration with impatience, or ignoring the emotional element altogether, leaves both server and served feeling badly bruised. And understandably, neither may be anxious for a repeat performance. Knock Your Socks Off Service professionals recognize the emotional element of a service breakdown and manage the recovery in a calm, professional, even-tempered way. To do that, it's not enough to just fix the problem. You also have to fix the person.

Color-Coding Your Response

Just as problems will have different solutions, fixing the person takes a different form depending on the "color" of your customer's emotional state. As a service professional, you've probably encountered it all, from coldly angry to frothing at the mouth. Some people seem very understanding when things go wrong, some make you feel absolutely terrible for playing a role in a service snafu, and others can instill a very real sense of fear in you.

We find it helpful to group customers by their reactions into three emotional colors: Blasé Blue, Ornery Orange, and Raging Red.

- *Blasé Blue customers.* These customers don't give you enough emotional clues to decipher their level of upset. For some, the service breakdown may simply be a nonemotional event—they roll with the punch and don't let it bother them. But be aware that seemingly neutral customers can move up the emotional scale if you don't take them seriously.
- *Ornery Orange customers.* Annoyed, these people exhibit mild irritation because their experience has fallen short of their expectations. Take them lightly or refuse to acknowledge their upset, however, and you can quickly escalate them to four-alarm fire status. Handle with care.
- *Raging Red customers.* These customers have major feelings of ire and frustration; they feel victimized and hurt by the service breakdown. Usually you won't have any trouble identifying their level of concern—it will be obvious to everyone within a three-block radius.

To see the differences among the three, consider how different repercussions of essentially the same initial situation, a late flight, can determine a customer's emotional color.

Blasé Blue. Bob's flight arrives one hour late, but he had a ninety-minute layover and can still make his next connection, so Bob's plans haven't been affected.

Ornery Orange. Olivia's flight is one hour late, causing her to miss a connection and to have to rebook on a later flight.

Raging Red. Ray's flight is one hour late, causing him to miss the last connection, resulting in an unplanned overnight stay and the need to call and reschedule a full day's worth of appointments.

Knowing the emotional color of your customer will help you choose the best people-fixing techniques. Here's a handy guide. If your customer is:

Blasé Blue

- Show surprise.
- Use general people-handling skills.
- Key into the customer.

Ornery Orange

- Show urgency.
- Enlist the customer in generating solutions.
- Create added value.

Raging Red

- Show empathy.
- Allow venting.
- Create calm.
- Listen actively.
- Plan follow-up.

Real problem solving cannot happen until the issues are out on the table. Blasé Blue customers often seem calm while "testing" your response. Show surprise and you demonstrate that this is not "business as usual"—and you pass the test. Fail to use good people-handling skills and watch this calm customer jump to Raging Red status. The tactics for Ornery Orange are designed to give this customer back a feeling of control and importance. Orneriness is often a substitute for fear or discomfort. Raging Red needs to be coaxed out of a temper tantrum.

Tip of the Iceberg

Fixing the person is an important element of a well-conceived recovery effort because many times a customer's emotional reaction is only tangentially tied to the real service problem. When you encounter an upset customer, you can't tell from the initial emotional readout whether their problem stems from a late flight, a broken radiator, a bounced check, or even, well . . . consider this illustration:

A friend of ours spent some years working behind the counter of an ice-cream store. One very busy day, a businessman came in and ordered a banana split. She made it, handed it to him, and went on to the next customer. Moments later, the customer was back: "This banana split has no bananas!" he hollered. "What kind of a moron makes a banana split with no bananas!!"

Stunned by the outburst, our friend could do little more than look at the man—and at the banana-less split. When he finally paused for a breath, she made the necessary effort:

"Gee, I'm awfully sorry about that. No bananas is a pretty serious offense in a banana split. I think I'd be upset, too. Please, let me make you a fresh one—and refund your money."

About that time, the customer became aware that he was ranting and raving over a bowl of ice cream, under the stares of the other customers and confronted by nothing more threatening than the sincere concern on a young woman's face. He started laughing. And she started to smile. And the other customers started to giggle and laugh. The upshot was that while she was making the new banana split, he apologized to her. And, needless to say, perhaps continued to be a regular at that ice cream shop.

> When a service tech goes on site, he has two repairs: He has to fix the equipment and fix the customer. And fixing the customer is more important.
>
> —Bill Bleuel
> Customer Satisfaction Consultant

30

Fair Fix the Problem

If you have trouble, it reduces the likelihood that the person is going to buy the next time.

—Joseph M. Juran
Founder of Quality Movement

Have you noticed that some people just seem naturally good at problem solving? No matter what the situation, no matter what the conflict, they are always able to see some course of action that will get the job done. Perhaps you are one of those people.

If you aren't, you may think, "I'll never be able to be as effective as they are—I don't have the talent." Wrong. Problem solving is a skill, not a talent. Effective problem solvers have simply learned to use their skills. To practice and hone your problem-solving skills, we recommend using a three-step framework: Listen—Probe—Solve.

Step 1: LISTEN to Find the Problem

The importance of good listening cannot be overstated. In a problem-solving situation, you are listening for two reasons:

1. To allow your customers to vent their frustration or irritation—part of the "fix the person" process.
2. To find the real problem (which may be obvious, but sometimes isn't).

For example, "listen" to this customer's complaint:

"I bought a Kid-Pro Bike from you people last night. The box must have weighed eighty pounds! I finally got it into my car—no help from you guys—and home, and it took me an hour to get it out of the car, into the house, and open. I mean really! This is a kid's bike and you need Arnold Schwarzenegger to open the box! And after all that, the directions were missing!! How am I supposed to put it together without the directions!?!"

TIP: Your customer has been practicing her little speech all the way to your store or office–don't deprive her of the right to deliver it, and in as dramatic a fashion as she likes. Even if you're sure you understand the problem–don't interrupt. You may be right, but you may not be. Listen until your customer is done explaining. She'll feel better for getting the whole story off her chest, and you may discover pieces of the puzzle you didn't even know were missing.

Upset customers are apt to bring multiple issues into their tirade. It's important to this customer that she had difficulty leaving the store, getting the box from her car to the house, and opening the box. But the immediate problem is the missing directions.

Step 2: PROBE for Understanding and Confirmation

Customers, particularly upset customers, don't always explain everything clearly or completely. Ask questions about anything you may not understand or need clarified. Then, when you feel you have identified and clearly understand the problem, repeat it back to the customer.

"I'm concerned about your purchase experience, and I'm going to share that with our manager. What I understand you need right now is directions. I've had that problem with assembling things myself, parts everywhere, with no directions in sight, and I know how frustrating it can be."

TIP: Use this step to make it clear that you agree that what the customer says is a problem really is a problem. Nothing annoys customers more than to hear a service representative respond to their concerns with an offhand "So?"

Step 3: Find and Implement SOLUTIONS

If the problem is one that you have encountered before, you may already know the best solution. In that case, use the "feel, felt, found" approach to present it:

"I can understand that you feel _____. Other people, including myself, have felt the same way. We've found that _____ solves the problem."

When the best solution is less obvious, present several options and ask for the customer's preferences.

"Fortunately, this doesn't happen very often. In those few cases when it does, I've found a couple of solutions that work. One is to check in the stockroom to see if we have another carton with a set of instructions in it. Or, if you're in more of a hurry, I can run a copy of the master copy we have. Which works best for you?"

Involving customers in generating solutions not only starts to rebuild the relationship, it gives them the feeling your business really is interested in satisfying their needs. You'll find that most customers bring a sense of fair play with them

and will often expect far less than you'd think. In our research into telephone repair services, for example, we learned that customers who experienced problems on the weekend didn't expect immediate service. They reasoned that telephone repair technicians wanted to spend weekend time with their own families, just like customers.

> **TIP:** If the solution you suggest is rejected by your customer or is met with a lukewarm reception, you may not be solving the real problem. Keep probing by asking what else your customer would like to see happen.

One Extra Step

Sometimes, solving the actual problem is not quite enough. Remember that the purpose of a Fantastic Fix isn't only to correct the problem, but also, and perhaps more importantly, to keep the customer. Rebuilding a damaged relationship, particularly when a customer feels victimized by the service breakdown, may require taking an extra step we call "symbolic atonement." It means making an appropriate gesture that says, "I want to make it up to you." Atonement is a way of providing a value-added touch to tell customers their business is important to you:

> "I'm glad you gave us a chance to make things right. Before you leave, let me write our store phone number on the directions. And since you had to make an extra trip, I'd like to give you one of these personalized bike license plates. What's your son's name?"

Don't fight, make it right.

—Hardee's complaint-handling policy

31

Customers From Hell Are Customers Too

There are no "bad" customers; some are just harder to please than others.

—Someone who never waited on a customer in his life

There is a world of difference between keeping your composure while working with an upset, angry customer who had a bad day in Consumerland and the burning sensation you get in your stomach when you come face to face with a fire-breathing, show-no-mercy, take-no-prisoners Customer From Hell.

Customers who have been *through* consumer hell need your help, support, and understanding. Those who come to you direct *from* hell need the special care and handling you might give a live hand grenade or an angry rattlesnake.

You would never tell the second group to their faces what you're thinking, "Oh no! Another Customer From Hell," but there's nothing wrong with admitting to yourself that this is what working with them feels like.

Customers From Hell play a simple game. Their goal is to get under your skin—to provoke you to counterattack. They taunt; you react; they win. If you lose control, you lose everything. Often, your first impulse is either to run and hide or to smack 'em. Or both. But you can't really do either. So, what do you do?

1. *Develop some perspective.* Real Customers From Hell are relatively few and far between. Most of your cus-

tomers want to deal with you in a cheerful, positive way. And even the really difficult ones are still customers.

2. *Remember that you are a pro. You* know your job and your company. *You* know your products and how they perform. And *you* know how to handle people, even when it's the end of the day, the end of the week, or the end of August and the air conditioning is broken.

3. *Be a master of the art of calm.* Let the upset and anger wash over you without sticking. Angry customers are almost never mad at you personally. They are mad at a situation they don't like.

Approaches to Obnoxious Customers

Our research with customers—and your stories of dealing with the most difficult ones—suggest four steps that, applied correctly, can calm the savage in the most beastly customer—most of the time.

1. *See no evil, hear no evil.* If you start thinking of customers as jerks and idiots, before you know it, you'll start treating them as badly as they treat you. Worse yet, you will start to treat the innocent like the guilty.

Mr. John Q. McNasty of the ABC Widget Company is the biggest jerk you have ever had to deal with. One day, you decide to fight fire with fire and be just as rude and insulting as he is. You give him a dose of his own medicine—and you feel great. John Q., of course, goes back to ABC and tells everyone what a stinker you are and that all *he* did was ask for a little service. Soon you begin to notice other ABC people acting up when you deal with them. And then, of course, you have to show these jerks that you can be just as tough as they are. And then. . . . You get the point, right?

Customers From Hell feed off your reactions. They use your response to justify their own behavior. Ignoring their rude and crude words and actions sends the message, "Slam,

bang, and cuss all you want. I am not intimidated." And that message, demonstrated, but not spoken, gives *you* the advantage.

> **TIP:** Don't try your company's Ten Commandments on Customers From Hell. Quoting rules or policy to justify your actions simply gives this kind of person something concrete to scream about.

2. *Surface the tension.* Some customers push your personal hot buttons through use of foul language or condescending tone. Others seem to direct their anger at you as if you were solely responsible for every woe in their lives. In fact, angry, temper-tantrum-throwing customers are so wrapped up in their emotions they often forget that you are a living, feeling person. "Surface the tension" is a way to gently remind them. Say: "Have I done something personally to upset you? I'd like to help. Please give me a chance." This will help return the customer's focus back to the issue, encouraging him or her to vent about the problem and not the person. The tag line, "Please give me a chance" is the real magic worker. We learned it from FedEx, where agents have long realized that it is a rare customer who won't, even if grudgingly, give you a chance. And

that's often all it takes to turn a frustrated customer from irate to angelic.

TIP: Worried that a customer's answer might be "Yes, as a matter of fact you have ruined my life"? It rarely happens, but if that is the answer, it's important to know why so you can correct the problem or misperception—or simply choose to move to the next tactic.

3. *Transfer transformation.* There *are* times when you are not obligated to continue a conversation with a customer. If you are personally offended, shocked, or dismayed by foul language, you have a right to deal with it. If a customer won't allow you to help him or her, you have an obligation to connect the customer to someone he or she will work with. Transferring the customer, be it to a peer or to a supervisor, is not a cop-out strategy. Instead, it is—if used in these situations—a clever, preplanned method for moving beyond a customer's negative, nasty behavior.

When you use it, you'll notice a strange, yet very human phenomenon. Consider what happens when Carol D. McNasty calls to inquire about a billing problem. You try to "surface the tension," but get "You imbecile! It's people like you who caused the fall of every great society! I want to talk to someone who actually has a brain!" So, you take a deep breath and put her on hold. You call your supervisor and explain the situation before putting Ms. McNasty's call through. Then you high tail it to your supervisors cubicle to watch her reaction when Ms. McNasty cuts loose. Instead, you see your supervisor smile and nod as she coos reassuring platitudes. Wait, it's worse! Your supervisor is actually laughing at something Mc-Nasty said! As she hangs up the phone, your supervisor turns to you and says, "What a character that McNasty is! Nice woman. What did you say to upset her?"

Are McNasty and your supervisor secret psychic twins? No. McNasty was having an adult temper tantrum. In putting her on hold, you put her in adult time-out. Just like those times you might use "time-out" with a small child, McNasty transitioned from her time-out to a different activity—in her case, speaking to a supervisor. She was able to leave her tantrum, and her terrible talk, in the past with you and make a fresh start in this new conversation.

4. *Build contractual trust.* What if McNasty doesn't quiet down? Or worse, what if a customer threatens you or begins to push and shove? At this point it is time to draw a line in the sand—but not one that forces your customer into the cold water of the river. Rather, you want to take your customer across a bridge and leave him or her on the far bank.

You are assistant maître d' at Chez Hot Stuff Café, the smartest, trendiest new restaurant in town. You are booked solid for the evening when the McNastys arrive with three friends and no reservation. Mr. McNasty takes you by the arm, leads you aside, and tells you that you *will* seat his party immediately if you know what's good for you. All the time he is talking, he is smiling—and squeezing your upper arm in an obviously menacing way. Make positive eye contact, smile right back, and say, "I'm sorry but unless we can find another way to have this conversation—a way that doesn't involve physical contact—I am going to have to call Security."

TIP: Use "I" statements like the one above. "You are a big bully who smells bad and probably has no friends," is bound to create resentment and defensiveness. "I" statements clearly communicate that you need the customer to stop a particular behavior—be it swearing or pushing—because, while others may find it okay, *you* can't accept that behavior.

You may have to repeat this phrase a second time, and then give him a moment to realize that you are serious. Then, if he stops, offer to put him on the waiting list. If not, say, "I'm sorry we couldn't find a way to work together." Call for your manager in a firm, *loud* voice. Then call 911.

Most customers will comply after you make the, "Stop this behavior and I'll help you; continue it and I won't" contract clear. If the customer doesn't comply, it's imperative that you follow through. This builds what psychologists call "contractual trust." In other words, you made a promise—"I'll call Security"—and you kept it.

Which tactic is best? Any of the four approaches can be correct in the right situation. Talk with your peers and your manager about when and how to apply each remedy to your difficult customers.

The customer isn't king anymore—the customer is dictator!

—Anonymous

32

The Customers From Hell Hall of Shame

They're only puttin' in a nickel, but they want a dollar song.

Country Song Title

Not all customers from hell are created equal. Some are masters of the slow drum. Others are top of their lungs screamers. Some beg. Some cry. Some threaten. A few even flatter. Our advice: Know Thy Enemy!

In our view there are FIVE types of Customers From Hell, which we now present to you.

Egocentric Edgar

Me first, me last, me only—that's his creed. You? You're just a bit player, an extra, an extraneous piece of scenery in that grandest of all productions: "Edgar: The Greatest Story Ever Told."

Sample Behaviors

Won't wait his turn, will only speak to whomever is in charge, intimidates through judicious name dropping, and makes loud demands.

Ways to Work With Edgar

- *Appeal to his ego.* Because Edgar is already a legend in his own mind, nothing soothes him faster than being acknowledged as a VIP. Simple things like remembering his name and using it can have a major impact.
- *Demonstrate action.* Edgar really doesn't believe that you can, or will do anything to help him. Taking some measurable, immediate action will go miles toward an amenable resolution of his problem—even if the problem exists only in his mind.
- *Don't talk policy.* Edgar does not want to hear about your company policy (as a matter of fact, no customer with a problem wants to hear about your company policy). Edgar expects to be exempt from any policies. Saying something like, "For you I can offer. . . ," and then offer whatever your standard policy is,
- *Don't let his ego destroy yours.* Edgar can be terrifically overbearing and his superior attitude invites the customer service person to feel unimportant. Don't take his self-importance as a personal affront. Focus on the business at hand, not on Edgar's disdainfulness.

Bad Mouth Betty

Her mother would be proud. Such an extensive vocabulary! It takes timing, talent, and a total lack of shame to swear like a trooper, but Betty makes it look easy.

Sample Behaviors

Uses language and has a demeanor that is caustic, crude, cruel, and foul.

Ways to Work With Betty

- *Ignore her language.* If you let her language get to you, then you've lost. Even though four-letter words are offensive, try to block them out. Remember she's really lashing out at the organization and not at you personally. Betty can often be defanged by asking, "Excuse, me, have I done something personally to offend you? Because if I have, I'd like to fix it or apologize." Betty is likely to stop in her tracks, say, "no," and tell you what she's really upset about.

- *Force the issue.* If Betty is swearing a blue streak, interrupt her and say, "Excuse me, but I don't have to listen to that kind of language and I'm going to hang up right now. As soon as you do that go immediately to your supervisor and say, "I just hung up on this customer for this reason." Research shows that most of the time (about 80 percent) the customer will call back and apologize.

- *Use selective agreement.* When Betty comes to you complaining about the outrageous waiting time in the teller line, agree with her! "Five minutes is a long time to wait, I can see why you would be upset."

Hysterical Harold

He's a screamer. If it's true that there is a child in all of us yearning to break free, Harold demonstrates the dark side of that happy thought. He is the classic tantrum-thrower, the adult embodiment of the terrible twos. Only louder. Much louder.

Sample Behaviors

Screams, is rabid and extremely animated, jumps around, and invades the personal space of others.

Ways to Work With Harold

- *Let him vent.* Harold has a lot of pent-up emotion. Let him wind down. Show Harold you accept his feelings, whether or not you agree with them, with neutral statements like, "I can see that you're upset," or "I don't blame you for being angry."

- *Take it backstage.* A public area is not the ideal location for Harold to explode. Walk him to a more secluded area like a conference room or private office. However, Harold may resist, thinking he's more likely to get his way if his tantrum is on display for other customers.
- *Take responsibility for solving the problem.* After Harold finally calms down, find out what the real problem is. Let him know that you want to and will do whatever you can to solve it.

Dictatorial Dick

Dick often shows up with marching orders. He issues ultimatums, sets arbitrary deadlines and tells everyone exactly how to do their jobs—after all, he "used to be in the business." And when his plan doesn't work? It's your company's fault, of course. Better still, it's your fault.

Sample Behaviors

Shows up with multiple copies of written directions or orders, insists on doing things his way, and suspects sabotage if things don't go his way.

Ways to Work With Dick

- *Break up his game.* Dick believes that getting adequate service from an organization requires going to war and striking first. If you treat him as if he is okay and say, "I'll be happy to take care of it for you," you break up his game. Nothing works on Dick like fulfilling his request promptly and accurately.
- *Stick with your game.* When you can't break up Dick's game or bend the rules, you can still play in good faith. Accentuate the positive by repeating what you can do for him.

Freeloading Freda

A material girl in a material world, she wants her dollar's worth—and yours, and mine, and anyone else's she can get. She doesn't make a game of getting more for her money—for her, it's a war.

Sample Behaviors

Wants something for nothing—or better yet—two for nothing, brings something back when it wears out, breaks, or begins to bore her, screams lawsuit or slander if accused of taking advantage.

Ways to Work With Freda

- *Treat Freda with the same courtesy and respect you would any other customer.* You can show courtesy and difference without giving away the store.
- *Find a fair response to Freda's complaint (fair in both your mind and in hers).*
- *You do not have to give in to Freda's demand.* However, giving in might be easier than avoiding the scene she's sure to cause with the other customers.

Look for the gifts—the things that every unpleasant encounter can teach you about dealing with ugly human behavior.

—Rebecca Morgan
Morgan Seminar Group

IV

Knock Your Socks Off Service Fitness:
Taking Care of *You*

We've focused our attention primarily on the customer. But there's another important player in the service game: *YOU!* A savvy service professional learns that self-management is every bit as important as managing the customer's experience.

Providing Knock Your Socks Off Service shouldn't be an impossible quest—or a personal ordeal. Like an athlete constantly in training, or a musician perfecting an instrument, you need to develop, evaluate, pace, and manage yourself as well as your performance. That means work, but it also means celebrating a job well done.

How you feel about yourself and the job you are doing—whether you love it or are overwhelmed by it—will inevitably be reflected in the quality of your work. Knock Your Socks Off Service should be rewarding for everyone involved.

33

Master the Art of Calm

The stress puzzle is the mind-body link: What roles do our emotions, thoughts, and perceptions play in the way we experience and physically respond to stressful situations?

—Dr. Frances Meritt Stern
President, Institute of Behavioral Awareness

You're not any good to anyone when you are stressed up, stressed out, overwrought, anxious, moody, belligerent, nasty, and still waiting for that first cup of coffee. The emotional labor involved in modern service jobs can actually be more draining than lifting boxes or pouring concrete. All the good stuff built into your job will never be enough if you don't learn how to cope with and counteract the stress.

In theme parks from Disneyland and Walt Disney World to Knott's Berry Farm, Universal Studios, and Six Flags, people at the front lines are taught the concepts of onstage and offstage.

- *Onstage* is anywhere a customer can see or hear you.
- *Offstage* is everywhere else, safely away from the public eye.

An employee who is feeling stressed can ask a supervisor to take over the ride operation, concession stand, or broom so they can get themselves back together. Once offstage, they can let their emotions out, deal with them, put their game face back on, and come back to the job without worrying about putting their next customer through the third degree.

You, your manager, and your organization have to work together to manage the environment in which you work. But only you can manage the way you react to a given service encounter. How do you cope? There are any number of techniques for reducing stress, whether inside your cubicle or out on the sales floor. Find those that work best for you and practice them every day. Here are ten to get you started.

Ten Stress Reducers

1. *Breathe.* Deep breathing is one of the oldest stress-busting techniques, and one of the best. Stress can upset the normal balance of oxygen and carbon dioxide in your lungs. Deep breathing corrects this imbalance and can help you control panic thinking. Take a deep breath through your nose—hold it for seven seconds (no more)—then let it out slowly through your mouth. Do this three to six times.

2. *Smile.* You make your mood, and your mood can stress or relax you. Smiling is contagious. When you see a customer looking a little glum, make eye contact and turn on one of your best and brightest. Ninety-nine times out of a hundred, you'll get a smile right back.

3. *Laugh.* Maintaining a sense of humor is your best defense against stress. Stress psychologist Frances Meritt Stern tells of a difficult client she had been dealing with for years. "That clown is driving me up a wall!" she often complained. One day, she began to envision him complete with white face, floppy shoes, and a wide, foolish grin. With this picture tickling her funny bone, she was able to manage her stress response and focus on doing her job.

4. *Let it out.* Keep your anger and frustration locked up inside and you are sure to show it on the outside. Instead, make an appointment with yourself to think about a particularly stressful customer later—and then keep the appointment. Unacknowledged tension will eat you up, but delaying your re-

action to stress-causing events can be constructive. It puts you in control.

> **TIP:** To get extra value from the technique, service representative Amy Gruber keeps a stress log of her most frustrating customers and situations. Adding an entry to the log helps calm her, and over several years the log has become a guide to dealing with her stress load.

5. *Take a one-minute vacation.* John Rondell, a sales consultant, has a vivid image of himself snorkeling off a beautiful white-sand beach in the Caribbean. He has worked on the scene until he can experience being there and lose all sense of time and place, even though his visits last only a minute or two. Now he can return to his "favorite place" following a stressful call or before talking to a stress-inducing customer.

6. *Relax.* We tend to hold in tension by tightening our muscles. Instead, try isometrics: tensing and relaxing specific muscles or muscle groups. Make a fist, then relax it. Tighten your stomach muscles, then relax them. Push your palms

against each other, then relax your arms. Some people get so good at it, they can do their exercises right under the customer's nose.

7. *Do desk aerobics.* Exercise is a vital component of a stress-managed life. Try these two "desk-er-cizes":

- While sitting at your desk, raise your feet until your legs are almost parallel to the floor. Hold them there, then let them down. Do this five times.
- Rotate your head forward and from side to side (but not back—that can strain rather than stretch). Roll your shoulders forward and then lift them up and back. This feels especially good after you've been sitting or standing for some time.

8. *Organize.* Organizing gives you a sense of control and lessens your stress level. "I organize the top of my desk whenever I am waiting on hold," says Eric Johnson, a telephone customer service representative. "Before I leave for the day, I make sure everything is put away, and that I have a list of priorities made out for the next day."

9. *Talk positive.* Vent your anger and frustration in positive ways. Sharing customer encounters with coworkers helps you find the humor in the situation and gain new ideas for handling similar situations. But constant negative talk that rehashes old ground will only re-create and reinforce, not diminish, your stress.

10. *Take a health break.* Change your normal breaks into stress breaks. Consider walking outside, reading a chapter from a favorite book, or just sitting with your eyes closed for a few minutes. Bring healthy snacks and juice to work to substitute for the standard coffee and donuts.

To paraphrase: You only serve as good as you feel. You need to take care of yourself. And you are the only one who can.

> When your customer is the most anxious, you need to be at your best—most competent, confident, calmest, and in control of yourself.

—Chip R. Bell

34

Keep It Professional

Every job is a self-portrait of the person who did it. Autograph your work with excellence.

—From a poster in an auto repair shop

Today, it's common to hear executives and managers proclaim, "Customers are our best friends." But Knock Your Socks Off Service professionals know that, for all the light banter and personal fanfare, there's a critical difference between being friendly and having a friendship.

A *friendly transaction* is a clear and understandable goal in any business—treating customers courteously, attentively, and professionally mimics the "transactional treatment" we would give to a close personal friend (and, in doing so, greases the wheels of commerce).

A *friendship,* however, is a relationship that begins and continues outside the bounds of the work we do and involves personal commitments far beyond the scope of the normal customer/server interactions.

Does that mean that customers should never be friends, or that friends shouldn't be customers? Of course not. We all hope our friends will chose to do business with us, and it's not unusual—and typically quite a compliment—when business relationships grow into interesting friendships.

If the letters to advice columnists are to be believed, it seems that a good percentage of today's romantic relationships grow out of service professionals meeting customers. But that's the result of a relationship that continues off the job.

Taking Care of Business

On the job, your customers are customers first and foremost: They have come to you not for conversation and companionship, but because they are trying to get their needs met through the business that employs you. Your customers need your help as a service professional, be it to ring up a sale, create a new hairstyle, or deliver five hundred pounds of industrial adhesive. They aren't there to look for a new friend.

> **TIP:** You are the most helpful when you remain professional, but with a personal touch. That means not confusing your off-the-job personal friendships with on-the-job, friendly, professional transactions.

It's worth noting that friendships can suffer some bruises when business gets in the way. Do your friends feel secure enough in your friendship to risk your displeasure if your friendly business services aren't satisfying? Even friends of longstanding may feel uncomfortable being honest with you in a business relationship that seems more a friendship than a professional partnership. They may withhold pointed feedback or suppress complaints, and ultimately may even take their business elsewhere, rather than create hurt feelings by telling you about their dissatisfaction.

Appearances also have an effect, both on customers who don't know you as well and on supervisors and coworkers who do.

- The next person in line may be made distinctly uncomfortable by the personal chatter and other evidences of a relationship that excludes them. Even though they may not be waiting any longer than normal, that wait will "feel'" longer to them if they think you could get to their needs more quickly by dispensing with what appears to them to be idle chitchat.
- Your coworkers and managers may have a similar reaction if they think you're giving unequal or preferential treatment to one particular customer, especially if there are other customers nearby to wait and watch.

Remember that a Moment of Truth for you and your business involves any time your customer has an opportunity to observe what you do and make a judgment on the quality involved. The best rule of thumb is to "keep it professional" at all times.

Involvement Varies

The difference between friendly and friendship and the difference between empathy and sympathy are related. When your friends experience pain or joy, you share those feelings with them. In that context, you sympathize as part of your friendship. When friends are in trouble, you may even offer advice. But it is not your role to fix everything for them.

When customers are upset, they expect you to care, too. But they also expect you to do something else that has nothing to do with a personal relationship: to fix their problem, to make things right, without becoming personally involved. Showing empathy as part of being professionally friendly is the best way to respect the difference between personal and professional conduct.

We conducted an informal poll of service professionals and customers, asking the question, "How can you tell that a

Table 34-1

Professional	Unprofessional
• Looks the part; neatly dressed	• Ignores you; usually in favor of a personal call or chat with a friend.
• Confident communicator; doesn't "uhm," and say "I don't know" without trying to find out.	• Sighs a lot; rolls his or her eyes.
• Smiles; looks eager to help	• Chews gum or eats while talking to you.

service provider is a professional? Table 34-1 reveals the most frequently given answers.

Who You Are vs. What You Do

There's another personal relationship that often gets over-looked by service professionals concentrating on doing their jobs to the best of their abilities: the one between you and those closest to you—your family and loved ones. During the course of the business day, you'll have many experiences and encounters—plenty of answers to the innocent question, "And how was your day, dear?" But while the stories you share can help your family better understand why you care so much about the work you do, it's unfair to overburden them with your professional concerns, just as it's unprofessional to violate the confidences of your customers.

> **TIP:** Draw a clear line between who you are and what you do—who you are goes home with you at the end of the day; what you do stays at work.

Good service is not smiling at the customer, but getting the customer to smile at you.

—Dr. Barrie Hopson and Mike Scally
Steps to Success Through Service

35

The Competence Principle:

Always Be Learning

You're never off duty; you have to remember everything you see.

—Holly Stiel
Concierge, Hyatt San Francisco

You've seen them. Maybe you've even worn one. You know, those little tags that say Trainee. The ones that proclaim to all the world, "Be patient, I'm still learning."

We often think of trainees as young, anxious to learn, full of questions—and as people who can't wait to take off the trainee label and finally know it all. But delivering Knock Your Socks Off Service means having a lifelong learning mentality. Learning your job doesn't stop when you turn in the Trainee tag. In fact, it's just beginning. Like professional athletes, the best customer service people are always in training, always looking for ways to improve their performance, always seeking ways to hone their service edge.

What do you need to know? Think of lifelong learning as a personal customer service workout program. Just as with any form of effective cross-training, your fitness regimen should cover several interrelated areas. There are five basics: technical skills, interpersonal skills, product and service knowledge, customer knowledge, personal skills. All are going to be critical to your success.

Use the questions below to test your strengths and weaknesses. You may keep your answers confidential so don't be afraid to be critical. At the same time, it's important to take credit for the many good and right things you already do.

Technical/Systems Skills

	No	Yes
1. I have the skills and training to use our telephone and communications technology.	☐	☐
2. I have the skills and training to use my computers and other technology in my work.	☐	☐
3. I know how to use organization systems and procedures to serve my customers.	☐	☐
4. When I need assistance using our technology or systems, I seek it in a timely manner.	☐	☐
5. I understand and can complete the paperwork required from my customers, and from me.	☐	☐

Interpersonal Skills

	No	Yes
1. I know the behaviors and attitudes that lead customers to say, "You really knocked my socks off!"	☐	☐
2. I can use specific techniques to diffuse angry or frustrated customers.	☐	☐
3. I can empathize with my customer's perspective.	☐	☐
4. I have insight into my own style and how best to respond to the styles of others.	☐	☐
5. I develop a feeling of partnership with customers and co-workers.	☐	☐

Product and Service Knowledge

	No	Yes
1. I can explain how my area's products and services contribute to my organization's overall success.	☐	☐
2. I can compare our products and services with those offered by our competitors.	☐	☐
3. I have the information I need about new or planned product and service offerings.	☐	☐
4. I know the technical terms and jargon, but I can explain in "plain English."	☐	☐
5. I know the most frequently asked questions, and the answers.	☐	☐

Customer Knowledge

	No	Yes
1. I know what customers complain about, and what customers compliment us on.	☐	☐
2. I know why customers choose us over our competition.	☐	☐
3. I know the "profiles" of my five most important customers/customer groups.	☐	☐
4. I know how the service I provide impacts the way customers rate us on quality measures.	☐	☐
5. I continually look for new ways to provide "Knock Your Socks Off Service."	☐	☐

Personal Skills

	No	Yes
1. I deal constructively with on-the-job stress.	☐	☐
2. I find new challenges and insights, even when doing "the same old thing" for customers.	☐	☐

	No	Yes
3. I organize and prioritize so I get the right things done, in the right order.	☐	☐
4. When faced with a customer's frustration or anger, I don't take it personally.	☐	☐
5. The work I am doing now provides an important step toward my long-term goals.	☐	☐

Learning Is Systematic

Keep a "learning log", a notebook or pad that's always near at hand, in which you write down both questions and answers that will help you better define your learning goals and improve your service performance. Organize your efforts: You can't learn everything at once, so don't try. Focus your lifelong learning program on one area at a time.

Put Yourself in Training

Use the space below or your Learning log to list five knowledge or skill areas that you would like to improve or add to your talent bank.

BUILDING YOUR TALENT BANK

1. _____
   _____
   _____
2. _____
   _____
   _____
3. _____
   _____
   _____

---

4. _____
   _____
   _____
5. _____
   _____
   _____

In the space below, identify two things you could do right now, without asking permission or investing a lot of money, to improve those skills. For example, you may want to ask a co-worker how she keeps her cool when customers burn red hot. Or you may ask to attend the next meeting of the local Society of Consumer Affairs Professionals (SOCAP), Alexandria, Virginia, International Customer Service Association (ICSA), Chicago, Illinois, or Chamber of Commerce to hear a speaker on customer service skills.

TWO THINGS I CAN DO RIGHT NOW:

1.

2.

Now, identify two things that would require greater effort from you and cooperation from others. For example, you may want to enroll in a local college to earn a degree. Or you may want to meet with your manager to find out how you can become an internal expert on your area's computer systems.

TWO THINGS TO EXPLORE FOR THE FUTURE:

1.

2.

Anyone who stops learning is old, whether at twenty or eighty. Anyone who keeps learning stays young. The greatest thing in life is to keep your mind young.

—Henry Ford

36

Party Hearty

You deserve a break today!

—McDonald's jingle

It's true. You do deserve a break today—and every day! It's important to take time out to celebrate your successes. Be good to yourself for doing a terrific job. No one else can celebrate as well as you can because no one else knows how well you've done.

If you've ever spent an hour or ten complaining about stupid customers or unsolvable problems—and who hasn't—remember the FCC rule of equal time. Spend as much time, or better yet, more time, rehashing your successes. From time to time, go out with your colleagues and celebrate each other for surviving and thriving in the work you do. Is it bragging about yourself? Sure. But there's no reason to downplay your skills and accomplishments. And recognizing your successes today will help motivate you to come back for more tomorrow.

Learning to Celebrate

Some people seem born knowing how to give themselves, and the people around them, needed pats on the back for work well done. But for most of us, celebrating ourselves doesn't come easy. We get so embarrassed when others start to sing our praises, we wouldn't even think of jumping in with a verse or two of our own. That's an attitude Knock Your Socks Off Service professionals can—and should—learn to leave behind. Give yourself permission to be terrific. That's right: You

175

need to make a conscious decision to allow yourself to occasionally revel in doing well. Once you do, we guarantee you'll learn to love the habit.

Still think it will be hard to get the hang of this positive feedback thing? Then start by practicing on someone else. Thank a colleague for helping you out. Make a point of letting your supervisor know something good about a coworker. Pass along a tip or trick you've learned from someone else—and make it clear who taught it to you.

Notice that these examples have a common element: They focus attention first on an action or accomplishment, then on the individual or team of individuals involved. In other words, you're not glowing all over someone just for being a wonderful person. Rather, you're taking note of what they did and why it was so terrific. Now start doing the same thing for yourself.

Five Ways to Celebrate

There are countless ways to observe and have some fun with your service successes. But take some advice from Yertle the Turtle. He tried to celebrate his own worth by rising high on the backs of his fellow turtles. It worked for a while, but eventually Yertle met the fate shared by all who lift themselves up by putting others down: He ended up face-first in the mud. Standing tall on the merits of your own service successes means celebrating personal victories, but it also means seeking out and celebrating the victories of your coworkers as well. Try these five ways to celebrate:

1. *Take yourself out to lunch.* Treat yourself to a special lunch or dinner or even breakfast. Invite a friend or coworker (or several) to go along and—this is the important part—make sure they know exactly what you are celebrating and why.

2. *Take a coworker out to lunch.* This one works the same as the one above, only this time the reason for celebration is a good service performance that has inspired you or given you added satisfaction or motivation in your job. Involving several

others reinforces the teamwork and camaraderie that makes good service organizations something special to be a part of.

3. *Buy balloons or flowers or something fun.* A balloon or fresh-cut flower on your desk can symbolize a recent service achievement. It also brightens up your work space and lets other people know you're feeling good about something. When they ask you, you'll have a chance to explain, which will make you feel even better.

> **TIP:** Consider giving the impromptu award you've presented yourself "legs." Enjoy it on your desk for a day, then pass it on to a coworker who just handled a Customer From Hell with grace and aplomb.

4. *Make a "brag sheet."* When you spend a lot of time working on the skills you'd like to improve, it's easy to forget to celebrate the strengths you already have. Start a list.

> **TIP:** When you have the inevitable bad day and are a little down in the dumps, pull out your brag sheet. It'll help put things in their proper perspective.

5. *Tell yourself, "You done good!"* Think talking to yourself is a little strange? It isn't. (Arguing with yourself, however, is a little suspect.) Good news gets better in the telling. If you're not quite ready to shout it from the housetops, at least tell yourself, verbally, with force and feeling, that you've done a good job.

> **TIP:** Be specific. Tell yourself exactly what you did well, better than you've ever done in the past. Then tell a co-worker, "You know, I just handled a really tough call and I left the customer feeling great." Or spread it around: "I watched you with that customer. She asked some pretty tough questions, but you had all the answers and sent her out of here feeling great. Nice job."

What gets rewarded gets repeated.

—Incentive and recognition axiom

Resources

To help you with your lifelong learning, here is a list of basic resources.

At America's Service by Karl Albrecht (Business One-Irwin, 1988).

The Complete Guide to Customer Service by Linda Lash (John Wiley and Sons, 1989).

Contact: The First Four Minutes by Leonard Zunin, M.D., with Natalie Zunin (Ballantine Books, 1994).

Customers As Partners: Building Relationships That Last by Chip Bell (Berrett Koehler, 1994).

Great Customer Service on the Telephone by Kristin Anderson (AMACOM, 1992).

"Helping Customers Cope With Technophobia" by Michael Ramundo (in MSM, January 1991).

"I'm First": Your Customer's Message to You by Linda Silverman Goldzimer (Rawson Associates, 1989).

Inside the Magic Kingdom: Seven Keys to Disney's Success by Tom Connellan (Bard Press, 1997).

Knock Your Socks Off Answers by Kristin Anderson and Ron Zemke (AMACOM, 1994).

Knock Your Socks Off Service Recovery by Ron Zemke and Chip R. Bell (AMACOM, 2000).

Moments of Truth by Jan Carlzon (Ballinger Publishing Co., 1987).

Netiquette by Virginia Shea (Albion Books, 1994).

Quality Customer Service by William B. Martin, Ph.D. (Crisp Publications, 1989).

Service America in the New Economy by Karl Albrecht and Ron Zemke (McGraw Hill, 2001).

The Service Edge: 101 Companies That Profit From Customer Care by Ron Zemke with Dick Schaaf (NAL Books, 1989).

Smart Questions: A New Strategy for Successful Managers by Dorothy Leeds (McGraw-Hill Book Company, 1987).

Tales of Knock Your Socks Off Service by Kristin Anderson and Ron Zemke (AMACOM, 1997).

Additional Resources

"Sox Off Service" videos starring Lily Tomlin, a four-part 1993 video series based on *Delivering Knock Your Socks Off Service*. Also, "On The Phone" videos starring Kristin Anderson, a six-part 1996 video series based on *Great Customer Service on the Telephone*. Videos are available individually or as a set through Mentor Media, Inc., Pasadena, CA.

About Performance Research Associates

Performance Research Associates (PRA), founded in 1972, consults with large and medium-size corporations and nonprofits on service quality, customer loyalty, and creating a customer-driven culture. PRA conducts organizational effectiveness and customer retention studies and creates customer retention strategies for a who's who of clients including Glaxo SmithKline, First Union Corporation, American Express Financial Advisors, PriceWaterhouseCoopers, Prudential Insurance, Harley-Davison, Bennington Capital Management, Dun & Bradstreet, CUNA, Wachovia Bank & Trust, Roche Diagnostic Systems, Oppenheimer Funds, Microsoft, Broadbase Software, General Reinsurance, Motorola, Universal Studios Theme Parks, Deluxe Corporation, and Turner Broadcasting System.

The firm currently has offices in Minneapolis, Minnesota; Dallas, Texas; Orlando, Florida; and Ann Arbor, Michigan. In addition to the company's consulting work, the firm's principals are heavily involved in writing, publishing, conducting seminars, and public speaking. Several of the principals make in excess of 100 paid presentations a year to business groups around the globe.

As a group, the PRA team has written more than fifty business books and several thousand articles. They have developed a dozen commercially successful, proprietary seminars, thirteen commercially available training films, and several proprietary organizational assessment instruments. The work of PRA partners touches hundreds of thousands of people a year in corporate America and beyond. To inquire about how PRA might assist your organization, please call 800/359-2576 or e-mail us at PRA@socksoff.com.

About the Authors

Ron Zemke is one of the leaders of the American customer service revolution. His writings and research on the organizational impact of customer service are considered landmark. Ron is the author or coauthor of thirty books including *Service America in the New Economy*, the entire *Knock Your Socks Off Service* series, *E-Service*, and *Generations at Work*. He is also senior editor of *Training* magazine, a syndicated columnist for the American City Business Journals, and acts as host in five films about the service management process.

In February 1994, Ron was named recipient of the Society of Consumer Affairs Professionals "Mobius" award for his contributions to the customer service profession. In March 1995, Mr. Zemke was named one of America's "New Quality Gurus" by *Quality Digest* magazine. In 1999, Ron was named the recipient of the Thomas F. Gilbert Distinguished Professional Achievement Award by the International Society of Performance and Instruction in acknowledgment of his significant contribution to the training and development field.

Ron is a highly sought after keynote speaker, workshop leader, and consultant who travels the globe sharing ideas and strategies for building strong relations with customers, partners, vendors, and employees. Ron can be reached at Performance Research Associates, Inc., 821 Marquette Avenue South, Suite 1820, Minneapolis, Minnesota 55402; telephone: (800) 359-2756; e-mail: PRA@socksoff.com.

Kristin Anderson, president of Say What? Consulting, is an internationally recognized customer service and communications expert. Through consulting, training, and keynote speaking, Kristin ensures that what employees say, do, and decide in the moment supports the service mission. Kristin coauthored four of the seven volumes of the *Knock Your Socks Off Service* series and is host of a six-part video training program titled, *On The Phone...with Kristin Anderson*. She is also author of *Great Customer Service on the Telephone* (AMACOM) and coauthor of *Customer Relationship Management*. She can be reached at Say What? Consulting, 2426 117th Street, Burnsville, Minnesota 55337; telephone: (952) 646-9283; e-mail: Kristin@KristinAnderson.com.

Index